Dr W. E. Shewell-Cooper is well known as one of the most
prolific writers on horticulture. As well as being Director of
the International Horticultural Advisory Bureau based at
Arkley in Hertfordshire, he has also made numerous
appearances on television and has written a great many
articles for newspapers and magazines. This book
embodies his highly successful methods in the form of a
straightforward and informative guide to cultivating and
cooking vegetables of every kind. By following his
principles and special tips, anyone, whether housewife,
vegetarian, or amateur gardener, can look forward to
achieving the very best results in the growing and cooking
of their own produce.

VEGETABLES

Vegetables
Growing and Cooking the Natural Way

Dr. W. E. SHEWELL-COOPER
M.B.E., N.D.H., C.D.H. (Wye), F.R.S.L., F.L.S.
Fellow and Doctor of The Horticultural College, Vienna

SPHERE BOOKS LIMITED
30/32 Gray's Inn Road, London WC1X 8JL

First published in Great Britain by George Allen & Unwin Ltd. 1975
Copyright © George Allen & Unwin Ltd. 1975
First Sphere Books edition 1978

TRADE
MARK

Printed in Great Britain by
Hazell Watson & Viney Ltd
Aylesbury, Bucks

Dedicated to my wife,

IRENE RAMSAY SHEWELL-COOPER,

who right from the beginning has been
my inspiration and my guide.

She and I together wrote the book
The Royal Gardeners at the request of
the late Sovereign King George VI
and she has helped me all the time
in the preparation of this book.

AUTHOR'S PREFACE

For many years now my wife and I have been the perfect team. I have grown the vegetables and fruit, and she has cooked and preserved them. In addition, I, myself, have always been interested in fruit and vegetable preservation, for as a young man I took a course on the subject at Chipping Campden (Bristol University), and, when Head of the Horticultural Department at the Swanley Horticultural College, I ran special courses for Women's Institute members on bottling, canning and the like, and we used to get 'full houses'!

As far as I know, this is the first real attempt at putting the two sciences and crafts (both are both!) into one book. My dear friend Eleanor Sinclair Rohde—who has since passed on—did lead the way in this field many years ago by including some recipes in her vegetable book—but now we hope we have included all the best recipes and have made both the compost growing and the necessary cooking appear simple and attractive.

May I thank all those who have encouraged us in this book, and especially Mrs. Rona Sillito who tirelessly typed the script.

W. E. SHEWELL-COOPER
Hon. Director

The Good Gardeners' Association
Arkley Manor
Arkley
Herts.
England

CONTENTS

ILLUSTRATIONS

CHAPTER ONE

The Importance of Growing Vegetables

The aim of this book is to encourage everyone who is able, whether they have large or small gardens, to grow more and better vegetables in greater variety, and having grown them, to harvest them correctly, to store them if necessary in the best possible way, and finally to cook them appetizingly in such a way that the maximum food value and flavour is retained.

Garden or allotment grown vegetables are superior in many ways to those bought from the shops. They are absolutely fresh with the maximum possible vitamin content and that incomparable and indefinable flavour which comes from their pristine crispness. By compost growing our own vegetables we can avoid the commercially produced vegetables which have been fertilized with artificially made chemicals, a point of great importance as our ecology consciousness increases.

Home grown vegetables help the housewife to economize, not only because they cost far less, but because there is less waste as there will be no limp leaves or bruised tissue to remove. One can gather the exact amount required when it is needed. The ready availability of fresh herbs in the garden is also important to the discerning cook.

Apart from the produce itself, there are several additional benefits from vegetable growing. It is a healthy and mentally relaxing activity in which the whole family can be involved and from which they can gain considerable satisfaction, and in a society which is increasingly aware of the need to conserve our natural resources and avoid pollution, the utilization of the land and the composting of all suitable rubbish will give an additional sense of achievement.

CHAPTER TWO

Non-Cultivation and Composting Methods

PREPARING THE COMPOST

The first thing to do is to establish a series of compost bins. I say 'a series' purposely, because the moment one bin is full and is capped with soil, the next one should commence. It is important to make the bin with wooden sides. In the normal garden 2 bins 4 ft. by 4 ft. should do; but with the larger country garden I advise making the bins 6 ft. by 6 ft. or even 8 ft. by 8 ft. In my own garden at Arkley Manor I have four bins 10 ft. by 10 ft. In each of these bins I can make 10 tons of compost.

When 2 or 3 bins have been erected side by side—preferably in a shady part of the garden and certainly with a level earth floor—it is possible to start collecting all the organic matter that is available. Do this day by day and week by week so as to fill bin No. 1. Remember anything that has lived should go on to the heap, and it is astonishing what comes under this heading, i.e. the tops of the peas and beans, the leaves of the beetroot, carrots, potato haulms, the lawn mowings and so on; the stumps of the brassicas (bash them up on a chopping block with an axe); the refuse from the kitchen—tea leaves, coffee grounds, fluff from the Hoover, fish bones and even old newspapers after they have been soaked in water.

As a matter of fact it pays to put these layers of newspaper in between two inch layers of lawn mowings as the mowings are apt to settle down too tightly, being very soft, and thus the air cannot get in. The aerobic bacteria thus cannot breathe and the anaerobic take charge and thus putrification sets in.

The moment there is a 6 in. thickness of refuse, apply an organic activator, a good fish manure, some seaweed manure, dried poultry manure or rabbit manure and all at 3 oz. to the square yard. If your land is acid (a B.D.H. Soil Indicator from the chemist will tell you this), then apply carbonate of lime at 6 oz. to the square yard at every fourth layer. If the organic material is dry, water it—but if it is damp (for instance, lawn mowings), don't! Eventually the heap will rise to a height of 7 ft. or so. It should now be capped with 2 in. of soil—like the crust of a cake—in order to keep the heat and moisture. Start now on bin No. 2 while the material in bin No. 1 is rotting down and forming the nice, eventually brown powdery compost to be used later.

Such compost making may not sound exciting; but it is the important beginning of all good organic vegetable culture. The gardener must start right. If you are a new gardener do not wait until the first bin of compost is ready, for nature has provided an excellent substitute known as sedge peat. Note this word 'sedge' because some firms are selling sphagnum peat and this isn't half as valuable. The medium grade sedge peat can be used instead of compost—it is in fact nature's own compost.

The material on the compost heap, whatever it may be, must be kept level all the time. It is well worthwhile, before going to bed, to go and see that the vegetable waste in the compost bin is quite flat and level. Stand on the vegetable waste and firm it while levelling. The bacteria must be able to work evenly right through the heap—fed of course by the activator. Thus a temperature of 180°F is ensured and this heat kills the weed seeds, the diseases and the pests. This, of course, is extremely important. At the end of the 6 or 8 months—6 months in the summer and say 9 months in the winter—the bulk of the material in the heap will consist of a lovely sweet smelling brown powder.

Any waste material in the front of the heap that hasn't been composted properly should be cut off with a sharp spade and should then go into the bottom of a new heap. Thus nothing is wasted. Don't attempt to put any woody material into a compost bin. This should be burnt. However, never burn any leaves or weeds or you will produce cancerous smoke. To burn wood, however, never produces cancerous smoke. This is significant.

Care should be taken to keep the heap moist—but never sodden. When making the wooden bins allow 1 in. between the planking so as to let air get into the heap, for the bacteria need to breathe. The reason the base of the heap must be soil is that the worms will burrow up when the heap is cool— they will go down again when the heap heats up—and up again a second time as the heap cools down. The worms are an important factor in good compost making.

The material when ready should be a dark brown powder. It may be almost black and should be free from an objectionable smell. It serves as a source of energy for the development of humus with the various beneficial organisms in the soil. The humus is said to be 'dynamic' and from the point of view of vegetables it certainly is. Humus is to the soil what human blood is to man.

Having ensured that plenty of living compost will be available for the garden, study the various methods of using it—and what other organic foods can be given to supplement what has been made available.

PREPARING THE GROUND FOR ALL VEGETABLES

Composting

The best way of preparing the soil in the vegetable garden or allotment under the organic gardening scheme is first of all to apply the powdery brownish-black compost all over the ground in October or November. Aim to give a dressing at least 1 in. deep so that this covers the soil completely. Don't dig it in—just leave it as a surface dressing.

Then in the spring a week or so before the sowing of any particular crop rotorvate the strip concerned with a light mechanical rotorvator or where this is not available fork the compost in an inch or so deep. The idea is to keep the compost as near the surface of the soil as possible and yet have a 'tilth' deep enough in which the seeds may be sown.

The part of the vegetable garden where the members of the Cabbage family are to be planted—the Sprouts, Cauliflowers, Kales etc.—need not be rotorvated for the plants may be set out at the right distance apart on the firm compost covered soil. Holes may be made with a dibber or trowel. When the soil was very hard on one occasion the author made holes for sprout plants with a 'crowbar' and the result was a very heavy crop!

The important thing is to continue year after year with this system and the soil improves season after season and the friable top soil deepens and becomes rich in organic matter. The weed population largely disappears and so less and less hoeing has to be done in the summer.

At the Demonstration Gardens of The Good Gardeners' Association at Arkley the vegetable garden is 120 ft. long and 85 ft. wide. The land itself is heavy sticky London clay with a thin layer of gravel on the top. Year after year for 11 years we have given this area 10 tons of compost each autumn, and today the whole of the area has on top of it a 2 in. or so layer of a fine easy worked organic matter—like soil. This is easy to cope with and it produces magnificent almost completely disease and pest free crops.

Mulching Organic matter, such as correctly made powdery compost or medium grade sedge peat, may be used all over the soil or merely along the rows of plants. This is ideal. If the roots of runner beans and peas are kept 'cool', for instance, heavier crops result. The mulches add organic matter to the ground and smother weeds at the same time. A complete mulch is naturally better than row mulching.

The Importance of Correct Manuring The food-producer should do everything possible to see that the soil that he cultivates is kept enriched with organic matter. The food value, the flavour, the quality of the vegetables, cannot be at a high level unless some kind of fully rotted and composted animal manure or vegetable matter is lightly forked in each season.

Organic matter assists in the aeration of the soil and helps to produce a better mechanical and physical condition. It provides the humus which is of course all important. Plants that are growing on land that has been enriched regularly with composted organic matter do not suffer as seriously from pests and diseases as plants growing on soil which is deficient in humus.

It is necessary, therefore, to add organic matter liberally each year and only to use organic fertilizers for stimulating the bacteria and for trying to supply deficiencies.

Farmyard Manure and Substitutes Strawy animal manures are not necessarily valuable, despite their content of organic material. They may contain diseases and are often full of weed seeds. Therefore, they must be composted before use.

Fresh animal manures when incorporated, may have a harmful effect, and it is vital, therefore, to see that they are incorporated in a compost heap for at least six months. Well-rotted composted manure is naturally far more valuable and is free from weed seeds, pests and diseases.

A good dressing of properly composted farmyard manure or compost would be one large barrowload to 10 sq. yds. each year. A compost heap 4 ft by 4 ft. and 6 ft. high should produce 4 tons of compost in about 30 barrowloads.

Seaweed Those who live near the seaside should certainly use seaweed. When rotted down it is most valuable. It should be used as a top dressing or mulch. It can be put on to the compost heap and be used with the vegetable waste.

Sedge Peat In the first place it may be as well to clarify the difference between sedge peat and sphagnum peat. Sphagnum peat is derived from the mosses, and sedge peat from the sedges and rushes. In our original work on the subject in 1950, we discovered that these two peats were quite different, both in composition and value—while in the experiments we carried out over several years, sedge peat always gave us better results. As to the use of sedge peat in the garden, it is undoubtedly advisable to use the medium grade. The very coarse type gets taken by the birds to make nests, and the very fine peat easily gets blown off the beds by the wind. When peat is used as a mulch it should go on at 1 in. deep all over the bed. This means that 1 cwt. of medium grade sedge peat will cover a bed of about 11 sq. yds.

Green Manuring Those who claim they cannot get hold of any of the organic substances mentioned, may add humus to their soil by means of green manure. This is obtained by growing plants and forking them in long before they come to maturity. Mustard, rape, rye, or vetches, are used, the seed being sown broadcast, and the plants that result are dug in two months later. Towards the end of the season, some gardeners sow all the seeds that they have left over and fork plants in that grow up *en masse* for green manure.

Before the green manure is forked in, it should be knocked about with a spade to break up the fibres. Then a fish manure should be applied over the mushed up green manure at 3 oz. to the sq. yd.

It should be noted in the normal way that ground to be green-manured has to be 'given up' to this system for at least two months.

Double Green Manuring Where land is full of perennial weeds and lacking in organic matter also, it should be forked over in the winter or early spring, and the seed of tares should be sown broadcast at the rate of ½ oz. to the sq. yd. In June the crop should be knocked down well with the spade and dried blood or fish manure applied at the rate of 3 oz. to the sq. yd. The material should be left for eight days after this, and should then be dug in shallowly. The surface of the soil should then be cultivated and sown with rye, this being incorporated shallowly after being chopped up with a spade —in October or November.

This system entails giving up the plot of land for a whole year, and should only be adopted where the ground is so foul with perennial weeds that it would be impossible to grow any vegetable crops.

The Use of Organic Fertilizers

Once the gardener has realized the importance of using organic manures, then he may supplement these with organic fertilizers—using them as a tonic, so to speak.

Nitrogen assists in building up the stems and the green leaves of the plant. When too much nitrogen is given, however, the plant's energies seem to be directed towards the production of leaves and rank shoots, with the result that its fruitfulness may be impaired. A plant over-fed with nitrogen is soft. Too much nitrogen defers ripening.

The most commonly used organic nitrogen fertilizers are:

1. Dried Blood. This is first class (if only it weren't too dear!). It can be used at 2–3 oz. to the sq. yd. for brassica crops, and is excellent for cucumbers also; and can be mixed with bone meal and wood ashes to form a 'complete' fertilizer.
2. Soot. This helps to darken light soils, and so enables them to absorb and retain heat better. It contains 1–6 per cent nitrogen only. It is generally used as a top dressing in the spring, at the rate of 5 oz. to the sq. yd.

Phosphates play their part with the roots. Crops grown on soil deficient in phosphates may ripen ten days or so later.

Phosphates help to produce that steady, firm, continuous growth that is more valuable.

The most commonly used organic phosphatic fertilizers are:

1. Steamed bone-flour, which is slow acting and so is used for the more permanent crops, like rhubarb and seakale, but is liked also by peas and beans. It is generally forked in at 2 oz. per sq. yd., some time in the autumn.
2. Bone meal, which is slower in action than the above manure, and cannot be expected to give as good results.

Potash plays an important part in the production of firm, well-flavoured vegetables. It is needed by all plants, which are healthier and better for its application owing to the strong fibre which results. Potash helps to give better colour. The sandy soils are normally deficient in this plant-food.

The main potassic food used by organic gardeners is wood ashes—useful if applied at ¼–½ lb. to the sq. yd. Coal ashes, however, can be very dangerous.

General Fertilizers

Fish Manure   This is valuable and is usually offered by the manufacturers free from objectionable odour. It is a 'manure' that rots down fairly rapidly and feeds the soil. Many manufacturers add potash during its preparation, and an ideal 'formula' is nitrogen 5 per cent, phosphates 8 per cent, potash 5–10 per cent. It should be used at about 4 oz. to the sq. yd.

Meat and Bone Meal   A slow-acting manure which contains 7 per cent nitrogen and 16 per cent phosphates but no potash, and is usually forked into the top 3–4 in. of soil at 4 oz. to the sq. yd.

Hoof and Horn Meal   Another slow-acting manure which contains 13 per cent nitrogen only and is applied as for Meat and Bone Meal.

Lime   Lime should be applied on the surface of the ground after the other manures have been lightly forked in. It is important, as it sweetens the soil and prevents it from being acid. It improves the texture and workability of heavy soils, adds calcium as a plant food, and, by helping to decompose manure and organic compounds, releases other plant-foods.

Regular applications of lime usually make it possible to keep at bay the club root disease. Lime is not so important for potatoes and roots as it is for cabbages and beans.

It is usual to apply hydrated lime at from 3–8 oz. to the sq. yd. Tests for acidity can be made with a Soil Indicator. Fellows of The Good Gardeners' Association can have their soils analysed free.

CHAPTER THREE

Cooking Vegetables Correctly

It is little use growing fine vegetables in gardens and allotments if the first-class produce is going to be spoiled in the cooking. This book is planned to help housewives to banish the eternal boiled potato and boiled cabbage, which seem to be the daily diet in so many households, and to teach the serving up of attractive and appetizing vegetable dishes. It is of great importance to grow as much as possible, and it is of just as much importance to cook properly what is grown.

Great care should be taken not to lose any of the goodness of the vegetables in preparing or cooking. For instance, the highest content of the valuable ingredients in the potato lies just under the skin, so that it should never be peeled thickly. Potatoes should, in fact, be cooked in their jackets whenever possible. The same principle applies to carrots and other root crops.

The water in which cabbage is boiled is a very valuable liquid, and should either be drunk or used for stock. A few people like to drink cabbage water at their meals, and it is useful in controlling rheumatism.

The modern steamer, with its several tiers, is a great boon, and a number of vegetables can be cooked at the same time by this method. Steaming is almost always better than boiling, and though the vegetables may have an 'unusual' colour, they will be richer in minerals, etc.

It will be seen from the recipes that there is no need to go in for expensive cookery to get the best results. The man or woman who cooks with care and intelligence is far more economical than the one who is 'slap-dash' and haphazard.

APPENDIX TO CHAPTER THREE

APPROXIMATE QUANTITIES TO ALLOW

Potatoes: 1 lb. is sufficient for 2–3 adults or 3 children (8–12 years).

Greens: 1 lb. is sufficient for 2–3 adults or 3–4 children (8–12 years).

Root vegetables: 1 lb. is sufficient for 3 adults or 4 children (8–12 years).

Soup: 1 pint is sufficient for 2 adults or 3 children (8–12 years). Where soup is served at a full-course meal, then 1 pint is sufficient for 4 adults or 5 children.

VEGETABLES IN SEASON

Name	In Season
Artichokes	October to May
Beans, broad	July to September
Beans, French	July to October
Beans, runner	July to October
Beetroot	All the year
Broccoli	October to March
Brussels sprouts	September to March
Cabbages	All the year
Cabbages, red	September to March
Carrots	All the year
Cauliflower	June to November
Celery	October to February
Haricot beans	All the year
Leeks	October to April
Onions	All the year
Onions, spring	March to June
Parsnips	October to May
Peas, green	May to October
Potatoes	All the year

Name	*In Season*
Savoys	November to April
Shallots	July to December
Spinach	All the year
Squashes	July to March
Turnips	All the year
Vegetable marrows	July to September

RAW VEGETABLES

Many vegetables are richer in food and vitamins when eaten raw. Further, the use of vegetables in their natural form makes it unnecessary to use heat for cooking. All forms of salads should, therefore, become the regular diet of every household. In far too many households the salad consists of lettuces, tomatoes, cucumbers, and radishes only. Fresh peas are excellent raw. Grated carrots are first-class. The hearts of large cabbages are very appetizing. Young French beans can be used.

Vegetables such as mustard and cress, water-cress and swedes should be grown more; the latter are also useful when grated.

MEASURES

'Cupful' referred to in the recipes means 1 Standard British cup (10 fl. oz.).

1 teaspoonful (British) = 5·9 ml
1 tablespoonful (British) = 17·7 ml
2 teaspoonsful = 1 dessertspoonful
2 dessertspoonsful = 1 tablespoonful

APPROXIMATE GUIDE TO OVEN TEMPERATURES

	Electric setting	*Gas mark*
Very cool or very slow	225°F	¼
	250°F	½
Cool or slow	275°F	1
	300°F	2
Moderate	325°F	3
	350°F	4

	Electric setting	Gas mark
Moderately hot	375°F	5
	400°F	6
Hot or quick	425°F	7
	450°F	8
Very hot	475°F	9

CHAPTER FOUR

The Family of 'Cabbages'

Under this heading I include all those crops, such as Brussels sprouts, cauliflower, broccoli, savoys, kale, etc., which are so important in our diet.

Fresh cabbage is rich in vitamins A, B1, B2, and very rich in vitamin C. All members of the cabbage family are perishable. It is therefore of great importance that they should be grown in all the gardens and allotments distributed throughout Great Britain.

All members of the cabbage family are subject to the club root disease, and it is advisable not to grow them on exactly the same piece of land for more than one year. The ground for this 'family' should be well limed if there is any tendency for it to be at all acid. 7–8 oz. of hydrated lime should be used per sq. yd., and this should be applied to the surface of the soil before the plants are put out.

BROCCOLI

This is a crop that should be grown only in districts where it is known to succeed well—such as the South or South-West. It is possible, by careful planning and sowing, to produce beautiful white curds of broccoli from the Michaelmas Day of one year to the middle of June the following year.

Soil and Manuring   Broccoli prefer firm soil, and should follow a crop that has been well manured. Light soils may have well rotted powdery compost applied at the rate of one barrowload to 10 sq. yds. over firm soil.

A good fish fertilizer with a 5 per cent potash content should be applied just before planting, at 3 oz. to the sq. yd.

Seed Sowing   The seed should be sown in drills $\frac{1}{2}$ in. deep, the soil tilth being fine. Most varieties can be sown during the second week of April, though the sowing of the June varieties may be delayed until the middle of May. Protect seedlings by means of black cotton, strung from short pieces of bamboo. The seed rows should be 9 in. apart.

Thin the seedlings out early, to prevent them from becoming too long and lanky. Transplant some of the seedlings to other beds 3 in. square if desired.

Planting   Plant after such crops as early potatoes, French beans, or even early peas. Distances apart: 2 ft. by 2 ft. Firm well after planting. Put plenty of water in the hole at planting time, should the weather be dry.

General Cultivation   Regular hoeing, and, if the winter is hard, the plants may be pushed over so that their heads incline to the North. If after this process the plants seem to flag, they should be given a good watering, unless the soil is in a condition to make this unadvisable.

Harvesting   The curds should be cut directly they are ready. If too many 'turn in' at a time, a leaf or two should be broken and put over the white heads. Another method of keeping them is to pull up the whole plant and hang it upside down in a shed.

Varieties

For Autumn: Veitch's Self-protecting.

For Winter or	Early Cornish for late December.
Early Spring:	Early Feltham for mid-January and the beginning of February.
	Roscoff, early February to end March.
	Cluseed St. George for April.
	Leamington for March.
	Markanta for May.

SPROUTING BROCCOLI

Sprouting broccoli should certainly be grown, for it is quite hardy, goes on producing those elongated flower-heads which are delicious to eat, and at the end of its season the leaves may be used also. By growing several varieties it should be possible to have plenty of greenstuff to cut at from late September until the beginning of April.

Seed Sowing   The seed should be sown in April, as advised for broccoli.

Planting   Put the plants out 3 ft. square when ready.

General Cultivation   Regular hoeing.

Harvesting   Cut the flower-shoots when they are found to be growing out in the axils of the leaves. Cut to within two-thirds of their length, and as a result more shoots will be thrown out on the same little stem. Do not cut the main leaves until all the sprouting tips have been consumed. It is the most economical crop to grow.

Varieties

Calabresse Green Comet: one of the earliest to turn in, and used in September. The shoots must be gathered regularly.

White Sprouting: cuts just before April and continues for many weeks.

Early Purple Sprouting: fit to cut in February and March onwards.

Late Purple Sprouting: stands the most severe frosts and yet 'gets away' immediately the weather is milder. Is excellent in April.

N.B. This vegetable has been proved to be one of the most valuable from the point of view of vitamin content, etc. Should be grown more.

BRUSSELS SPROUTS

These should not be grown unless there is a good deal of land available. They like a long season of growth, and cannot be hurried. They can, however, produce heavy crops when properly treated.

Soil and Manuring Sprouts like firm land. A well piled barrowload of powdery, composted vegetable refuse should be put on to cover every 8 sq. yds. In addition, fish manure should be sprinkled over the compost at 3 oz. to the sq. yd. If the plants are not growing satisfactorily after they have been put out into their permanent position, dried blood may be applied at 1 oz. to the yard run.

Seed Sowing The main sowing should be done early in April in a finely prepared seed bed. The drills should be $\frac{1}{2}$ in. deep, 9 in. apart, and the seeds should be sown thinly. The plants that arise should be transplanted 6 in. square in another border before they get leggy.

Sowings can also be made in frames early in March, or in a sheltered border the previous year in September.

Planting The plants should be put out 3 ft. square, during May or early June.

It is advisable to inter-crop between the rows in order to make the utmost use of the ground, and so spinach, radish, or lettuce should be sown in between.

General Cultivation Remove the large leaves of the plants as they begin to turn yellow. Keep a look out for the blue fly or aphis, and dust vigorously with derris if any signs of it appear.

Harvesting To make the most of sprout plants, cut off the sprouts with a knife, leaving a short stalk on the main stem. Do not break them off. The little short sprout stems will then throw out further open sprouts, and this second crop is often of great value.

Cutting should be done systematically from the bottom of the stem upwards.

Varieties

Peer Gynt: wonderful flavour—easy to pick early.

Improved Ormskirk Giant: good for the North. It grows tall and is a very heavy cropper.

Irish Elegance: mid-season—high quality sprouts—medium size—smooth.

Sanda: the mid-season type, producing large, firm sprouts, excellent for the deep freeze.

Cambridge Late No. 5: the late type of the same series and just as good as the earlies and maincrops.

CABBAGES

There are spring, summer and winter cabbages, apart from the savoys, which will be dealt with under a separate heading. There should be no difficulty in keeping up a supply of this excellent vegetable all the year round.

Soil and Manuring Cabbages will grow on almost any soil, providing the ground has been fed with properly composted vegetable refuse. This powdery refuse may be applied at the rate of one barrowload to 10 sq. yds. In addition, fish manure or meat and bone meal will be used at 3 oz. to the sq. yd. During the growing season dried blood may be applied at 1 oz. to the yard run, if it seems necessary.

Lime should be applied to the surface of the ground before the plants are put out if, after a test, the soil is found to be acid. Hydrated lime is generally used at from 5–7 oz. per sq. yd.

Seed Sowing For spring cabbage—these are the cabbages that are cut in April and May—the seed should be sown late in July. The seed bed should be prepared as for broccoli, the seed being sown in drills 9 in. apart and ½ in. deep. Sow the seed thinly and there is no need to transplant.

For summer cabbage, the seed should be sown in March.

For winter cabbage also, March sowing is desirable, and a second sowing, if necessary, early in May.

Planting Spring cabbages should be planted after such crops as early potatoes, peas, or beans, during the month of September. The plants should be 12 in. apart, with 18 in. between the rows.

Summer cabbage should be put out when the plants are ready and whenever the land is free—18 in. by 18 in.

Winter cabbage should be put out 3 ft. by 3 ft.

General Cultivation The spring cabbages should not be given any nitrogen in the autumn, or they become too soft to live through the winter. They should be given dried blood in early March at the rate of 1 oz. per yard run to hurry them along.

Summer and winter cabbage are often put out during dry weather, and should therefore be well watered in.

In all cases the rows should be hoed regularly, except that the spring cabbage should not be hoed during the wet winter months.

Harvesting Cut the cabbages directly they are ready to use, but do not leave the stalks in the ground, or they will foul the land. Smashed up, they can easily be rotted down, with fish manure, on the compost heap.

Varieties

Spring Cabbage:	Cluseed First Early, No. 218: probably the earliest variety of cabbage known. It forms a good heart.
	Harbinger, which follows the above: the hearts make delicious eating.
Summer Cabbage:	Primo: a round head which cuts in July and August.
	Winnigstadt: a conical variety for August and September.
Winter Cabbage:	The Swift: grows well, is compact, and has a pointed heart.
	Christmas Drumhead: a later variety which grows very large.
	January King: a very late excellent variety.

CAULIFLOWER

This crop will give good results if properly cultivated and is very popular.

Soil and Manuring The soil should be covered with powdery compost at the rate of one good barrowload to 8 sq. yds. Just before planting out, fish manure should be given, as advised for cabbage. Finally, lime should be applied to the surface of the ground if, after a soil test, it proves necessary.

Seed Sowing To get an unbroken supply of good white curds from early June to the end of November, it is necessary to sow seeds at various times of the year.

An autumn sowing is made late in August or early in September, and the plants thus raised are pricked out into frames 4 in. square, where they live throughout the winter, to be planted out early in March in a sheltered part of the garden. January and February sowings can be made in boxes placed in frames or greenhouse, and when the young seedlings come through, the plants are pricked out 4 in. apart into further frames. These plants are put out early in April. Another sowing is often made out of doors late in March or early in April, in rows 6 in. apart, the seedlings being thinned out to 3 in. apart in the rows, when they are well through. Still later sowings may be made late in April or early in May in a similar manner.

Planting The autumn sowings are often planted early in March in a sheltered position, 1 ft. square.

For the later sowings, the rows are usually 2 ft. apart, the plants being 18 in. apart in the rows. For the late summer sowings the rows should be 2½ ft. apart, the cauliflowers being 2 ft. apart in the rows. Plants should always be put out before they get too big, as in this way better crops result.

General Cultivation During dry weather copious waterings should be given.

When the plants are 'curding', i.e. producing their white curds, one or two of the inner leaves should be bent over the flower to prevent it from turning yellow.

Harvesting The curds should be cut as early in the morning as possible. If too many heads turn in together, the plants may be pulled up with soil attached to the roots and hung up in a shed, as advised for broccoli.

Varieties

Autumn Sowing: Orion: an early type, well protected by foliage.
All the Year Round: compact grower.
Cluseed Major: an early type, producing large, well rounded heads.
Unwins Snowcap: turns in about seven days later than Cluseed Major—is suitable for spring and summer sowing.
Dominant: comes to maturity about the same time as Snowcap and produces large heads.

January and February Sowings:	Salvo: similar to All the Year Round.
Spring Sowings:	Majestic: a fine cauliflower, comes into cut in the late summer and early autumn.
Later Sowings:	Improved Autumn Giant: produces huge white heads.
	Polar Bear: cuts in Nov.–Dec. Solid white heads.

1 Surplus cauliflowers can be stored by hanging them upside-down by their roots in a shed.

KALE

The kales are invaluable in a severe winter, for they ensure
a good supply of green vegetables throughout the cold
months. Instead of being harmed, they are improved by
frosts.

Soil and Manuring   There is no need to make special
preparations for kales, as they should follow another crop. If
this is impossible, they may be manured as advised for
cabbage.

Seed Sowing   This is done the first week in March in the
South and towards the end of March in the North.
   A fine seed bed in an open situation should be prepared
by raking the soil down well. The drills should be 9 in. apart,
and if the plants have to be thinned and transplanted, they
should be put out 6 in. square.
   Asparagus kale seed may be sown as late as June and July.

Planting   The plants should be ready to put out into their
permanent positions at the end of June or the beginning of
July. They are a useful crop to follow early potatoes, early
peas, lettuce, spinach, or French beans.

General Cultivation   See that the plants have plenty of
water to start with. If dry, pour water in the holes at planting
time.

Harvesting   Allow the kales to grow and build up a good
plant, then keep cutting at them. Early in the New Year the
heads of the kales may be removed, and then dozens of side
growths will break out. These are first-class for food.

Varieties

Cottagers' Kale: will withstand the most rigorous winter.
Dwarf Green Curled: a robust compact variety. Leaves
densely curled.

Hungry Gap: an excellent late kale. Lives through any hard winter.

Asparagus Kale: a hardy late variety. Can be sown where the crop is to be grown.

Thousand-headed: very hardy, strong, and branching. Excellent for use in the spring.

SAVOYS

These can be regarded as a winter cabbage, and, like the kales, are improved by frost. They are well worth growing because of their hardiness.

Soil and Manuring   Likes to be grown on firm ground, and is excellent to follow a crop like early potatoes or peas.

The soil should be prepared as advised for sprouts. In addition, a good fish fertilizer may be added at 3 oz. to the sq. yd.

Seed Sowing   The seed should be sown in three batches: the first during the third week of March, the second at the beginning of April, and the third at the end of April.

The drills should be 9 in. apart, and directly the seedlings appear they should be thinned out to 3 in. apart. These thinnings may be transplanted to further beds, 6 in. square, if desired.

Planting   The plants may be put out into their permanent position at the end of June and during the month of July. In the case of the smaller varieties the rows should be 18 in. apart and the plants 15 in. in the rows. With the stronger varieties, 3 ft. square is advised.

Harvesting   Cut directly the hearts are of a good size, and remove the stalk from the ground directly the savoy has been cut, as advised for cabbages.

Varieties

Best of All: excellent for cutting in September and October.

Omega: cuts from November to February—very hardy.

Ormskirk Late Green: cuts from January to end March. Stands the most severe weather.

Savoy King (F1 Hybrid):   cuts from February or March.

CHAPTER FIVE

Cooking the Cabbage Family

Continental cooks are always making fun of the soggy boiled cabbage which they regard as part of the Englishman's daily diet.

Actually, there is a lot of truth in this criticism, for as a race we are lax in the way we cook our 'greens'. Often they are so unappetizing that children, in whose diet they are essential, can only be persuaded to eat them with bribes or threats. Here are a number of recipes to make them attractive, more palatable, and, because they are properly cooked, richer in vitamins and food value.

Special Note: Some people complain that cabbage is indigestible. A good way to make it digestible is to pour off the water when it is half cooked and place the cut up cabbage into another saucepan of fresh boiling water.

BROCCOLI
(See Cauliflower, p. 51.)

SPROUTING BROCCOLI

Bundled

Cut off the flowering heads before the flowers open and tie them up into bundles of a dozen or so. Steam these, or else place in a stewpan with a little margarine and cook in a moderate oven, with a cover on. Remove the string of the bundles before serving.

Loose

Steam, or boil, in a very little water in an earthenware dish, drain for some time in a warmed colander, and serve with a little melted margarine. Never over-cook sprouting broccoli, or it falls to pieces.

BRUSSELS SPROUTS

Boiled or Steamed

These are one of the few greens that are better boiled than steamed.

Pick off any dead or yellowing leaves from the outsides; wash well in some salted water, and allow to stand for half an hour. Place the washed sprouts into a saucepan of boiling water, adding a tablespoonful of salt. Boil quickly until tender, drain well in a warmed colander, and serve in a warmed vegetable dish, sprinkled with a little salt and pepper and a dash of butter or margarine if desired. It is important to serve this vegetable hot, for it cools quickly.

Stewed Brussels Sprouts

Prepare the sprouts as for boiling. Place in a deep fireproof dish, adding two tablespoonsful of hot water to each ½ lb. of sprouts. Place a tablespoonful of butter or margarine in the middle. After covering over, place in a hot oven until tender.

Sprout Omelette

Clean and boil some sprouts and see that they are really tender. Drain well through a warm colander. Cut up finely and place into a bowl. Drop in the whites and yolks of two eggs and beat or whisk together well. Season with pepper and salt.

Place a little margarine, butter or dripping in a frying-pan, and when really hot, pour in the egg-and-sprout mixture and fry until brown. Serve while hot, with slices of lemon.

Cheesy Brussels

Boil some sprouts in a little water and when tender drain in a colander. Place them in a pie-dish at least two layers deep and pour over them a thick white flour-sauce. Sprinkle over the top, two or three tablespoonsful of grated cheese and add three or four small pats of butter or margarine. Place into a hot oven and bake until light brown.

Variations of this dish are possible: for instance, mashed boiled chestnuts may be mixed in with the sprouts before covering with the sauce, or cold diced cooked ham can be used instead.

CABBAGE

Boiled Cabbage

The dead outside leaves should be picked off and the hard part of the stalk cut away. If large, the cabbage should be cut into quarters, and if small, the stalk should be criss-crossed with a sharp knife. If there is any fear of insects, soak for half an hour in a basin of water to which a dessertspoonful of salt has been added. Wash well in clean water, and then place in a saucepan filled with boiling salted water. Boil rapidly with the lid off until the cabbage is tender. Time taken, about half an hour.

When tender, take out, place into a colander, and press with the underside of a saucer. Drain thoroughly, serve in a warmed vegetable dish, either chopped up well and seasoned with pepper and salt and a pat or two of margarine, or, if the cabbage is small, cut into portions, placing a tiny pat of margarine in the centre of each.

Steamed Cabbage

Steamed cabbage may not look so attractive, as much of the colour goes, but the true cabbage flavour is retained, and so are the valuable salts. It should be served in the same way as boiled cabbage, with a little melted margarine or butter.

Cabbage Soup

Choose a white cabbage, wash it well, cut it up into four, and allow to soak for an hour in water to which a dessertspoonful of salt has been added. Rinse it in fresh water, and shred it up finely. Put a little margarine or butter in a saucepan and add the shredded cabbage, stirring it until it has absorbed the margarine or butter. Then pour in a cupful of water and heat until cooked.

Peel some potatoes—two large ones to one large cabbage is the right proportion—and slice them up very finely. Add them to the cabbage, together with a little more water. When cooked, mash the cabbage and potato together, add a glass of milk, and boil. Serve hot, seasoned with pepper and salt.

Creamed Cabbage

Steam or boil a cabbage and, when cooked, cut it up finely. Make up a sauce consisting of 2 oz. of margarine or butter, 2 oz. of flour, and a pint of milk, and season with pepper and salt. Mix the cabbage with some of the sauce—just sufficient to moisten it—and place in a greased fireproof dish. Arrange on the top, sections of sliced hard-boiled eggs and, if available, sliced tomatoes. Pour on the remainder of the sauce and sprinkle over the top three tablespoonsful of grated cheese. Add a few dabs of margarine or butter and bake in a moderate oven, until brown.

Chestnut Cabbage

Prepare the cabbage as for boiling, and cook in boiling salted water for 15–20 minutes. Strain well in a colander and chop up finely. At the same time prepare a cupful of chestnuts, boiling them until tender. These should then be peeled and also chopped up finely. Mix the cabbage and chestnuts together, add a teaspoonful of margarine or butter, a cupful of gravy, mix well and serve hot.

Stuffed Cabbage

A nice round cabbage should be selected, and, after being thoroughly washed, the leaves should be turned back, one at a time, and the stuffing placed in position in a layer. It may consist of minced beef or, better still, minced pork, together with a little onion chopped up finely and seasoned.

When stuffed, the cabbage should be tied up fairly tightly and placed in a steamer for three-quarters of an hour. When cooked it is delicious if served with tomato sauce.

Cabbage and Cheese

Prepare and clean a cabbage in the usual way. Put into a saucepan of boiling salted water and boil quickly. When turning soft, place into a colander to drain, and then chop up with a sharp knife and season with pepper and salt.

Place the cabbage, after pressing tightly, into a fireproof dish, and grate plenty of cheese and breadcrumbs over the top. Dab with a little margarine or butter and bake in a moderate oven until brown. It may be served with a little white sauce, and is particularly delicious if, before placing the cabbage in the dish, two rashers of bacon are placed in the bottom.

Paprika Cabbage

> *1 large tender cabbage*   *½ tablespoonful paprika*
> *3 tablespoonsful butter*   *1 teaspoonful marjoram*
> *Pepper and salt*

Cut the cabbage neatly into eighths. Put into a basin of very cold water for six minutes to crisp leaves. Lift out—drain somewhat. Put three tablespoonsful of butter in a large saucepan and melt on a flame. Now add the cabbage as it is with some icy water still on the leaves. Sprinkle with the paprika, powdered marjoram, pepper and salt, and cover with a tight lid. Put over a low flame and simmer. You must allow the water on the cabbage to turn to steam and then it will cook without being burnt. (In a pressure cooker, by the way, the cabbage only takes three minutes to cook.) Serve with a little more melted butter and sprinkle with more paprika if you like your dishes 'hot'.

Buttered Cabbage

1 young cabbage	*3 teaspoonsful chopped basil*
3 tablespoonsful butter	*Pepper and salt*

Cut the cabbage into quarters or eighths, according to its size. Soak in cold water to crisp the leaves. Drain. Melt the butter in a heavy pan and put the wet cabbage into it. Season, cover tightly and bring to simmering point over a low flame in order that the cabbage is able to form enough steam to cook without burning. Cook until tender for about ten minutes. The liquid should not be thrown away: thicken with cornflour and serve with the cabbage. Add milk and a little butter if preferred.

Bacon-Stuffed Cabbage

1 large savoy or cabbage	*1 cup breadcrumbs*
6 rashers smoked bacon	*2 eggs*
½ lb. lean bacon, minced	*Pinch of mixed herbs*
2 onions	*Pepper*

Strip the outer leaves from the cabbage and wash them. Blanch them in hot salted water for ten minutes, then drain and dry them. Peel and chop the onions and fry until just brown. Chop the cabbage heart finely and add to the onions. Season with pepper and herbs and fry gently for eight minutes. Leave to cool. Mix well together the minced bacon, crumbs and beaten eggs. Line a heatproof dish with the bacon rashers and blanched cabbage leaves. Put the bacon, breadcrumbs and other ingredients in the centre, cover with the rest of the rashers and bake in a moderate oven, say 350°F, for 1½ hours.

New England Boiled Cabbage

1 cabbage	*6 lb. piece of ham*
6 potatoes	*6 onions*
6 young turnips	*Mustard sauce*
6 young carrots	

Soak the ham overnight, then bring to the boil and simmer for three minutes. Drain, put in fresh water and simmer for one hour. Peel the turnips, carrots and onions and plunge them whole into boiling water for a minute, then add to the ham. After fifteen minutes, cook the cabbage and potatoes in the same way, add to the ham and boil gently until the potatoes are done. Lift the ham on to a dish and arrange the strained vegetables round the outside. Serve with mustard sauce.

British Sauerkraut

Make it in the autumn or winter, because it needs a large cabbage and cool weather.

Wash and shred the cabbage very finely. Put two breakfast cupfuls in the bottom of an earthenware jar with a lid, and sprinkle with salt. Repeat until the jar is full, then pour on cold water until it is just visible. Cover and leave in a cool place for two or three days, by which time it will have fermented. Press with a wooden spoon now and then so that the cabbage may be only just above the water. It is now ready to eat. The juice is palatable, especially when mixed with the same quantity of tomato juice.

Cabbage Pie

1 large cabbage	*6 large tomatoes*
2 oz. margarine or butter	*1 onion*
Pepper and salt	*Cupful of breadcrumbs*

Boil or steam the cabbage. Peel the tomatoes and grate the onion. Put in a greased fireproof dish layers of the cabbage leaves, tomatoes, and onion (double the quantity of cabbage to onion and tomatoes). Dab with small pieces of margarine or butter after covering with a layer of breadcrumbs about ½ in. thick. Bake in a quick oven until thoroughly heated through and lightly browned.

Dutch Cabbage Pie

1 medium sized cabbage	*2 beaten eggs*
½ teaspoonful salt	*Pepper to taste*
1 tablespoonful melted butter	*2 tablespoonsful thick cream*

Trim off the outside cabbage leaves. Wash, drain and shred the leaves well. Put them into boiling salted water. Boil until tender, then drain. Mix in the eggs, butter, pepper, salt and cream. Pack all into a greased shallow fireproof dish. Bake in a moderate oven for twenty minutes. Serve with any cold meat you wish.

Bubble and Squeak

Mix together the left-over boiled potatoes and boiled greens and season with pepper and salt. Place a little dripping in a frying-pan and when hot put in the potato-and-greens mixture pressing this down evenly. Cook until the bottom is brown.

This dish is much improved if an egg or two can be spared to be beaten up and mixed with the vegetables before frying.

Cabbage and Apple Vegetable Dish

¼ lb. onions	*1 oz. dripping*
1 lb. cooking apples	*½ pint of water*
2 lb. cabbage (trimmed, washed, and finely shredded)	*Pepper and salt*

Melt the dripping in a saucepan, add the onion which has been thinly sliced, and also the peeled, cored and cut-up apples. Fry this mixture gently for four or five minutes without browning. Add the cabbage, water, a teaspoonful of salt, some pepper and the sugar. Cover the pan and cook for an hour until vegetables and fruit are well merged together and the liquid almost absorbed. Season to taste and serve hot.

Cabbage and Apple Salad

½ lb. tender white cabbage	½ cup of thick salad dressing
½ lb. apples	½ lb. even-sized tomatoes,
1 teaspoonful finely	skinned and sliced
grated onion	Chopped parsley

Shred the cabbage finely and wash and dry; peel the apples and grate. Add the onion and half the salad dressing and season if necessary. Pile some of this in the centre of the salad bowl, arranging the tomatoes round the bowl, and then pour the remainder of the apple-cabbage mixture in carefully.

RED CABBAGE

Most people think of red cabbages as useful only for pickles, but they are very delicious when steamed or boiled, and red cabbage is *the* vegetable to serve with game!

Red Cabbage Steamed or Boiled

Prepare and cook in the same way as advised for ordinary cabbage (see p. 44).

Red Cabbage Stewed

Steam or boil a red cabbage until half-cooked, and then cut up into slices and place in a pan. Grate over it a little fresh onion. Add a dessertspoonful of margarine or butter, season with pepper and salt, cover with a lid, and cook until tender.

Red Cabbage Salad

Shred up a red cabbage raw and place in a bowl. Pour over a cupful of vinegar, two tablespoonsful of salad oil, and sprinkle with a tablespoonful of salt and a teaspoonful of black pepper. Mix well together and allow to stand for two days before serving. The cabbage is thus softened and absorbs much of the dressing.

Ham Delight

Prepare the cabbage exactly as for stewed red cabbage, only, in addition, when putting the cabbage into the dish to cook, add two slices of ham cut up finely, with a dessertspoonful of vinegar and ½ pint of good gravy stock.

If desired, this dish can be served with sausages laid round.

CAULIFLOWER

(N.B. All recipes given for cauliflower are also suitable for broccoli).

Cauliflowers can be eaten raw as well as cooked, and they are delicious in salads when grated. It is the flower-head that is so wholesome and rich in vitamins.

Boiled Cauliflower

Prepare and clean as for cabbage. Place into boiling salted water, flower side downwards. Boil for five minutes, remove scum, and turn the flower side up, sprinkling with a little sugar. Continue boiling for a quarter of an hour. Remove carefully, place in a warmed vegetable dish and cover with a thick white sauce. Garnish with chopped parsley.

As an interesting change this vegetable may be served with a cheese sauce or with a tomato sauce.

Boiling to Ensure Serving Whole

Wash, clean and prepare the cauliflower, and plunge whole, flower side upwards, into cold water and bring to the boil. Remove the cauliflower and plunge into dead cold water for two or three minutes. Then place in boiling salted water for a quarter of an hour to twenty minutes. Cauliflowers cooked this way never break.

Cauliflower Fritters

Take some cooked cauliflower, mash, and add a little flour to thicken. Mix with one egg and enough salad oil to make into a cream. When smooth, add milk to make into a batter. Season with pepper and salt.

Fill a small saucepan three-quarters full of dripping, and when boiling drop in the thick batter spoonful by spoonful. Fry until golden brown. Serve in a heated vegetable dish. Excellent with mutton.

Cauliflower Soup

Prepare two small cauliflowers, cooking them in boiling salted water until tender. Drain off the water, placing this in a small container. Chop up the cauliflower finely. Season with salt and pepper, cover, and stand on one side. Boil the water in which the flower has been cooked, putting in 2 oz. of crushed tapioca. Cook slowly. Mix 1 oz. of ground rice with ½ pint of milk and add this to the cauliflower in the bowl. Mix together well and pour gradually into the saucepan in which the water and tapioca are cooking, stirring all the time. The soup should then be brought to the boil and served at once.

Cauliflower Salad (i)

Grate the uncooked flower of a cauliflower and mix with an equal quantity of grated radish. Serve with chopped, crisp fresh lettuce, garnishing with parsley. A thick mayonnaise sauce improves it.

Cauliflower Salad (ii)

Cut up the cauliflower into small portions. Cut tomatoes into slices. Slice cold young potatoes and crisp lettuce leaves. Mix together, cover with mayonnaise sauce, and garnish if possible with a little chopped hard-boiled egg.

Cauliflower and Cheese (i)

Clean and prepare a cauliflower. Boil it as if to serve whole, and when cooked and drained well, stand in a greased fire-proof dish. Make up a thick white sauce and stir in plenty of grated strong cheese. Season with salt and pepper and pour the mixture over the cauliflower. Bake in a moderately hot oven until golden brown. Serve hot.

Cauliflower and Cheese (ii)

Boil the cauliflower and, when cooked, cut up and place in a greased fireproof dish with alternate layers of finely grated strong cheese. Pour a thick white sauce over the top and sprinkle more grated cheese over this. Place on top a few pats of margarine or butter and bake in a moderate oven until brown. Serve hot.

Cauliflower au Mushroom

1 large cauliflower	1 tablespoonful butter
6 mushrooms	1 oz. breadcrumbs
¼ pint grated cheese	1 pint cream sauce
Salt and pepper	½ teaspoonful minced parsley
1 teaspoonful capers	A pinch crushed herbs

Boil the cauliflower in salted water until tender. Drain well. Remove the centre stalk and a portion of the stem. Place in a fireproof dish into which butter has been melted. If it is too high for your dish, or if you haven't a dish deep enough to take it, cut a thin slice off the top, for it must be level. Mix the breadcrumbs with capers, mushrooms, herbs, parsley and cheese, well chopped up. Pack the stuffing into centre of the sprigs, after moistening it with some sauce. Sprinkle thickly with extra cheese. Bake in a moderate oven for about twenty minutes, or until brown.

To make the cream sauce, follow any recipe for ordinary white sauce, but substitute cream for half the milk suggested.

Curried Cauliflower

Boil the cauliflower and cut up into small portions. Into half the water in which the cauliflower was boiled, place one large cut-up apple. Boil this until soft, and then put in with it a tablespoonful of sultanas. In a small basin, mix a dessertspoonful of curry-powder with a tablespoonful of flour.

Moisten to a cream with a little water, place in the saucepan with the apple, and stir continually over a low heat to thicken. Last of all add the cauliflower previously cooked. Serve in the centre of a ring of rice which has been cooked in quickly boiling salted water for a quarter of an hour.

Stuffed Cauliflower

Place a cooked cauliflower, flower side up, in a greased fire-proof dish. Remove the centre of the flower and put aside for use on a future occasion. Fill the hole thus made with minced cooked beef, seasoned to taste, and cover the whole with a thick brown sauce. Place in the oven for half an hour to heat right through the centre, and serve hot with fingers of toast.

Cauliflower Fondue

1 cauliflower	*3 eggs*
2 oz. butter	*3 sprigs parsley*
2 oz. flour	*1 tablespoonful seasoning*
½ pint milk	*3 tablespoonsful brown*
2 tablespoonsful grated cheese	*breadcrumbs*

Break the cauliflower into sprigs. Put the butter and flour in a pan, add the milk, and heat up. Stir briskly over the fire until boiling. Add half of the cheese and season to taste. Beat in the egg yolks and then the stiffly whipped whites. Put a layer of this in the bottom of a pie dish, well buttered, and then a layer of cauliflower. Repeat as required, finishing with a layer of soufflé mixture. Sprinkle with brown breadcrumbs mixed with the rest of the cheese, add a few dabs of butter, and bake for half an hour in a really hot oven. Sprinkle with chopped parsley.

Cauliflower, Tomato and Cheese Salad

1 large cauliflower	*3 lumps sugar*
6 medium tomatoes	*Salt and pepper*
3 oz. grated cheese	*Salad cream*

Soak the cauliflower in cold water to which a tiny piece of washing soda has been added. Rinse and wash thoroughly in two waters before plunging it into salted and sugared boiling water and cooking until tender. (Sugar does help to bring out the flavour of the vegetable, and keep it white). Drain the cauliflower and allow it to get cold, then divide into small sections. Arrange these in a pile in the middle of a salad bowl. Add the grated cheese, season with salt and pepper. Cover with the tomatoes, preferably skinned and sliced. Serve with ample salad cream.

KALE

Kale can be cooked in the same way as advised for cabbage.

The fresh young leaves may be used in salads, and are richer in food value than lettuce. They are excellent in the winter-time when lettuces are scarce. Curly Kale is particularly tender.

CHAPTER SIX

Root Crops

The root crops are important because they will keep. They provide very excellent food, not only during the late summer and autumn months, but also in the winter. Most of them are rich in vitamins A, B_1, B_2, and C.

The parsnip is particularly useful, because it can be left in the ground until required, and so takes up no storage room at all. Moreover, parsnips give nearly three times as much heat calories as swedes.

BEETROOT

Beetroot may be grown quickly to be used during the summer or sown to be harvested in the autumn and stored. They are not only excellent when used cold as salad, but are first class when boiled or steamed and served hot; they also make excellent fritters.

Soil and Manuring   Beetroot grow best on a lightish soil, though they can be grown in almost all gardens.

Seaweed has proved an excellent manure for beetroot, and may be applied at the rate of a barrowload to 8 sq. yds. Finely divided composted vegetable refuse may be used instead at the same rate. A good fish fertilizer is excellent for beetroot if applied at 3-4 oz. to the square yard. The potash content of the manure should be 10 per cent.

The long beetroot do well on land that has carried celery or leeks the previous year.

Seed Sowing The seed should be sown at the end of April or the beginning of May. The rows should be 15 in. apart and the drills 2 in. deep. In the North, delay until May 15th if necessary.

Very early crops may be obtained on a sunny South border by sowing at the end of March, in rows 1 ft. apart. Protection should be given to the young seedlings with black cotton or fish-netting, against birds. The drills in this case are only $1\frac{1}{2}$ in. deep.

Another sowing of an early variety may be made in July, so as to obtain fresh young roots in the autumn and winter.

Thinning and transplanting Thinning should be done when the plants are 3 in. high; first of all to 4 in. apart, and then, when the roots are the size of golf balls, to 8 in. apart. These 'golf-ball' thinnings may be eaten.

Young beetroot thinnings may be transplanted if gaps should occur, but a good watering must be given every day afterwards until the plants are well established.

General Cultivation The rows should be hoed regularly and the roots should never be damaged, for if they bleed the colour is lost.

Harvesting Beetroot may be left in the ground until they are needed in the winter, providing the rows are covered with straw, bracken, etc. to guard against severe frost. Usually they are lifted and stored in a clamp, as advised for potatoes (see p. 102). The tops should be cut off before storing, but this should never be done too near the crown, or bleeding may take place. It is possible to store in sand or in dry earth

in a shed, and the roots will keep until the following
June.

Varieties

Round-shaped: Show Bench: a good, dark, round type.
Very delicious—excellent colour.
Boltardy: Bears globe-shaped beets, which
when cut through are free from disfiguring
white rings. Doesn't go to seed.

Long-shaped: Exhibition Crimson: deep red—small top.
Cheltenham Green-top: Green-leaved.
Uniform long roots.

Intermediate: Spangsbjerg Cylinder: excellent flavour—
half long and half round. All the advantages
of both.

CARROTS

By various sowings of early maturing varieties and by the
judicious storing of main crops, it is possible to have carrots
all the year round. They contain about 9 per cent of carbohydrates.

The shorthorns and forcing types should be grown in warm
borders and in frames; the intermediates are often used as a
main crop, especially on heavier soils, while the long types
give the heaviest weight and do extraordinarily well on
deep, sandy soil.

Soil and Manuring   Carrots prefer a deep, well-cultivated,
sandy loam, and heavy soil used for carrot growing should
be improved by the addition of sandy or gritty material. On
clays the shorter-rooted types should be grown.

Before sowing the seed, the soil should be well raked level.
Fish manure should be added at the same time at the rate of
4 oz. per sq. yd.

To hurry along early crops, fish or seaweed manure may be

applied at the rate of 1 oz. per yard run, at fortnightly intervals until the roots are half grown.

Seed Sowing   A very early sowing may be made on a sunny South border or other warm spot in March, in drills 6–9 in. apart. Protection may be given to the rows by means of cloches, sacking, or frame-lights.

The normal sowing will be made in April, in drills ¾ in. deep and 12–18 in. apart, according to the variety. To ensure thin sowing, mix a little dry earth with the seed beforehand. Another sowing may be made in July. In this case the seed is sometimes broadcast instead of being sown in rows.

Thinning   If the early sowings have been done properly, there should be no need for thinning. The roots should be pulled early, while they are young. The same advice holds good for the July sowing.

During the last five years I have not thinned the main crop sowings either. The sowing has been done thinly and because of the heavy dressings of compost year after year, the carrots have grown to a good size without any thinning being done. Further, by not thinning—the Carrot Fly maggots are not seen.

General Cultivation   To ensure quick germination, it is advisable to give the rows a flooding from time to time. After this, all that needs to be done is to hoe regularly.

Harvesting   Before the winter frosts, the roots should be lifted and stored in sand or dry earth in a shed, the tops being cut off first of all. If preferred, the roots may be put into a clamp, as described for potatoes (see p. 102).

Varieties

For a Heated   There is nothing better than Demi-longue
Frame (or over   à forcer.
a Hot-bed):

For the Cold Frame:	Sweetheart, produces small, almost cylindrical roots.
For the Early Border:	Early Gem, a stump-rooted variety, or Primo.
For an Ordinary Main Crop:	New Scarlet Intermediate is first class.

PARSNIPS

This is one of the easiest vegetables to grow, and should be cultivated on a much larger scale. It is rich in food value, it keeps well in the ground, and its only disadvantage is that it likes a long season of growth.

It is nice steamed or boiled, served with white sauce. It is first class parboiled and baked in beef dripping, and it is excellent fried.

Soil and Manuring Parsnips will grow in almost any soil. Gardeners who have difficulty in getting long, straight roots, owing to stony ground, should bore holes with an iron rod, 3 ft. deep and 3 in. in diameter at the top, and 1 ft. apart; and fill these up with sifted soil. Three seeds can then be sown on top of each, the seedlings being thinned out to one if all grow.

This crop should be grown on land that has been well composted. Meat and bone meal or a good fish manure may be applied as a top dressing a few days before seed sowing, at 5–6 oz. per yard run.

Seed Sowing In the South the seed should be sown at the end of March, and in the North towards the middle of April, providing the land is not too wet.

As the seed does not germinate well, it may be sown rather more thickly than carrots. The rows should be 18 in. apart and 1½ in. deep.

2 As parsnip seeds germinate slowly, they can be sown mixed with faster germinating lettuce seeds to mark out the rows. The lettuces should be thinned out so that the plants grow alternately.

Mixing the seed with plenty of lettuce seed is a good idea. Thus the lettuce seedlings mark the rows early. I thin out so as to leave a parsnip, a lettuce, a parsnip, a lettuce and so on. You thus get a natural intercrop.

Harvesting As has already been said, the roots may be left in the ground until required. If there is any danger of the ground being frozen so as to prevent the roots being dug up, a certain number of them may be lifted and stored in a clamp. Under ordinary conditions a little litter placed over the rows will prevent them being frozen.

Varieties

For Shallow Soils:	Avon Resister: a heavy cropper. Resistant to Parsnip Canker.
For Deeper Soils:	Improved Hollow Crown: has a clearer smooth skin.
	The Student: good in the North, where later sowings are made.

SWEDES

Garden swedes are valuable because they are so hardy in the winter. They are more delicate in flavour than the turnip, and have a calorific value of 145 per pound. They contain 7 per cent of carbohydrates and 2 per cent of fibre.

Soil and Manuring Will grow on almost any soil. Light land should be enriched with an organic fertilizer, such as meat and bone meal, hoof and horn, or a good fish manure, applied at 4–5 oz. per sq. yd. and raked in a few days before seed sowing.

The surface of the soil should be limed with hydrated lime at the rate of 4–7 oz. per sq. yd., depending on the acidity of the soil. Test for acidity before sowing.

Seed Sowing The seed should be sown in drills 18 in. apart. In the South the seed is usually sown in May, and in the North, early in June.

Thinning Thin out to 1 ft. apart when the plants are 2–3 in. high.

General Cultivation In very dry seasons flood the rows from time to time. Hoe regularly and dust, if necessary, with derris dust every two or three days to keep down the turnip flea-beetle. This is usually at its worst when the plants first come through.

Harvesting Like parsnips, the swedes may be left outside throughout the winter and dug up as desired. They are, for this reason valuable, as they take up no storage room.

Varieties

Purple-top Field Swede: clean, well-shaped roots of good colour.

Garden Swede: said by epicures to be the better flavour.

TURNIPS

Turnips may be grown as a main-crop to be used in the winter, or there are the tennis-ball-sized types of turnips which should be cooked when young. Indeed, it is possible to keep up a supply almost all the year round. Turnips are not as valuable as swedes, for their calorific value only stands at 95, and their carbohydrate value at 4 per cent as against 7 per cent in the case of swedes. To diabetics and slimmers the lower calorific values can be important and advantageous. Many people however, do not care for the flavour of the swede.

Soil and Manuring Turnips will do well on almost any soil except a shallow one. On a dry droughty soil the roots have a tendency to run to seed and are usually badly attacked by the flea-beetle.

The top of the soil should be enriched with sedge peat or powdery composted vegetable refuse at 1 lb. to the sq. yd., and, in addition, a good fish manure, meat and bone meal, or hoof and horn may be given at 4–5 oz. to the sq. yd.

Seed Sowing   There are four periods when the seed may be sown:

1. *In the Frame:*   In February or March sow the seed in holes made 1 in. deep and 4 in. apart each way. Drop four seeds in a hole and thin out to one if all grow. After sowing, fill in the holes. The frame should be heated, or over a hot-bed. Turnips will not stand a great deal of forcing, and the frames should be given as much ventilation as possible from the time the seedlings are through.

2. *Outside Early:*   A sowing may be made in the early part of March if the ground can be got down to a fine tilth. The rows should be 4 in. apart and 1 in. deep. The seedlings should be thinned out to 4 in. apart. Another sowing may be made in April, the drills being 12 in. apart, the plants being thinned to 6 in. apart when they are 1 in. high.

3. *The Main Sowing:*   The main sowing is usually done in May—if possible in a shady situation. The rows should be 1 ft. apart, the turnips thinned out to 6 in. apart. The roots from such a sowing are pulled in the late summer.

4. *Winter Turnips:*   Seed should be sown any time from the middle of July until the end of August, the drills being 18 in. apart, and the plants thinned to 6 in. apart when 2 in. high. When the thinnings are fit to use, a further thinning should be done to 1 ft. apart.

General Cultivation   A sharp look-out must be kept for the turnip flea-beetle, especially in the early stages, and regular dustings with derris and pyrethrum dust should be given.

In dry seasons it may be necessary to give a good flooding once a week or so. Regular hoeings are also necessary.

Harvesting   Pull the spring- and summer-sown varieties

while they are young and fresh, and before they get coarse.

The main crop turnips may be dug up in the autumn, before the sharp frosts occur, and should be stored as advised for carrots and potatoes.

Winter turnips may be left outside until needed for use.

Varieties

For the Frame:	Selected Early Snowball: a pure white.
Early Outside:	Early White Milan: a pure white, or Early Snowball.
Main Crop:	Golden Ball: a yellow-fleshed garden turnip. Orange Jelly: a similar variety.
Winter Turnip:	Chirk Castle: the flesh is firm and white.

TURNIP TOPS

The green leaves of the turnip tops are very useful as a vegetable, and will be of the greatest value in winter, when greens are scarce.

Another great advantage is that this vegetable may be sown late—i.e. early in September—for use in late February, March, and early April.

The rows should be 2 ft. apart, and the seed should be sown thinly. No thinning should be done, and the crop should be allowed to grow naturally.

The leaves should be pulled as required, and though good roots are not to be expected, it is sometimes possible to use some of the roots that develop when the leaf part of the crop has been harvested.

KOHL RABI

(See p. 186)

SALSIFY

(See p. 187)

CHAPTER SEVEN

Cooking Root Vegetables

Roots are very useful indeed, because they can be used during the wintertime, when other vegetables are scarce.

BEETROOT

Too many people use beetroot only as a salad, cold and sliced and in vinegar. It makes an excellent hot vegetable, providing young roots are used. Older roots can be used, but they take much longer to boil and are not quite as tender.

Boiled Beetroot

Wash the roots under a tap until quite clean; be sure that during this process they are not bruised, or they will 'bleed', and that will spoil the look of the vegetable when it appears at the table. Boil slowly for about two hours, and, after removing the skins, place in a hot vegetable dish. Pour over the beetroot a thick white sauce with a little melted butter or margarine put into it right at the last. The young beetroot may be served whole, but the larger ones should be cut into four before being served.

They can be steamed instead of boiled, but this process takes about half as long again.

Beetroot Soup

Boil the beetroot as advised above, peel, and cut up into dice. Put into a pint of milk and a pint of water and bring to the boil, and simmer until the beetroot is soft enough to mash. Season with pepper and salt and serve hot.

As a change, a little chopped celery may be mixed with the beetroot.

Beetroot Salad (i)

Slice cold cooked beetroot and put neatly in a glass dish. Put a ring of chopped celery around and grate a little horse-radish on the top. Serve moistened with a good salåd dressing.

Beetroot Salad (ii)

Instead of using celery, use thinly sliced onion in a ratio of two parts of beetroot to one part of onion.

Stuffed Beetroot Salad

3 large beetroot	*2 apples*
2 hard-boiled eggs	*½ pint vinegar*
1 bunch watercress	*4 oz. sugar*
6 pickled onions	*2 teaspoonsful seasoning*

See that the beetroot are of good shape and even size before boiling them until tender. Cool a little, peel and cut into pieces at least 2 in. long. Remove the centre of each portion to form an egg-cup shaped hole. Cover the beetroot with vinegar and leave for one hour.

Shell the eggs and chop up fine. Mix with the chopped pickled onions, apples and a spray or two of watercress. Season with salt, pepper and castor sugar. Drain the beetroot from the vinegar, place on a dish; pile the chopped mixture into little pyramids in each beetroot. Just before serving, surround with the remaining watercress.

N.B.   These three salads are a pleasant alternative to the well-known method of just slicing boiled beetroot and serving it in a dish of vinegar.

Hors d'Oeuvre

Beetroot when cooked and diced are often used in hors d'oeuvre mixed with a mayonnaise sauce.

CARROTS

It must be remembered with root crops, and especially with carrots, that the valuable minerals and salts lie immediately under the skin. It is therefore inadvisable to peel thickly; it is better, in fact, to cook them in their 'skins' and to scrape them afterwards.

With carrots, the best flavour will result if the roots are pulled out of the soil just before they are to be used in the pot. This is, of course, impossible in the depth of winter, but is advisable during the summer and autumn.

Steamed Carrots

Wash the roots thoroughly and put them whole into the steamer, where they will take about $1\frac{1}{2}$ hours to cook if on the large side.

Boiled Carrots

Place in cold water to which some salt has been added and bring to the boil slowly. Boil until tender.

Quick Boiling

Cut the carrots into very thin rings and cook in a saucepan with a very little water. The lid of the saucepan must fit very tightly.

Minced Carrots

Wash the carrots and put them through a mincer, using the coarsest cutter. Place this mince in a fireproof dish and season with pepper and salt. Dab with one or two pats of butter or margarine and add a tablespoonful or two of hot water. Cover with a lid and put into a moderate oven until cooked.

Carrot Custards

> *1 pint grated carrots*   *1 tablespoonful butter*
> *2 egg yolks*   *Salt and pepper to taste*

Melt the butter in a pan. Add the carrots. Fry slowly for ten minutes, stirring constantly. Beat up the egg yolks. Season with salt and pepper to taste, and stir into the carrots. Pour into small buttered individual moulds. Place the moulds in a baking tin. Pour in enough hot water to cover the tin $\frac{1}{4}$ in. deep. Cover the 'custards' with greased paper or aluminium foil. Bake in a moderate oven for about fifteen minutes until set. Stand for a moment or two, then turn out.

Carrot Soup

> *6 medium-sized carrots*   *1 onion*
> *$\frac{1}{2}$ head celery*   *1 oz. margarine or butter*
> *$\frac{1}{4}$ lb. bacon*   *$\frac{1}{2}$ oz. cornflour*
> *1 saltspoonful sugar*   *$\frac{1}{4}$ pint milk*
> *1 quart stock*

Chop up finely the carrot, celery, and onion. Mince the bacon. Put into saucepan with the margarine and simmer for half an hour. Add the stock and cook for another hour. Strain off the vegetables and pass through a sieve, returning to the saucepan. Mix the cornflour with a little milk to make a smooth cream, and add to the pan, bringing the contents to the boil. Lastly, add the remainder of the milk and season with pepper and salt. Should be served very hot.

An alternative to this soup is the use of turnip instead of celery and the use of vegetable liquor instead of stock. The sugar in either case should be added just before serving.

Carrot Pie

Boil the carrots whole, skinning them afterwards. Mash to a pulp and add a little grated onion in the proportion of 1 of onion to 8 of carrot. Mix well together, adding at the same time 2–3 oz. of margarine or butter. Place the mixture into a pie dish and bake for half an hour in a hot oven. Pour over a hot, thick white sauce to which an egg and a dash of lemon-juice have been added. Put back into the oven for about a quarter of an hour.

Carrot Pudding

Boil or steam the carrots whole and when tender remove the skins and rub through a sieve. To each ½ lb. of carrots used, dust over ¼ lb. of sugar and cream with ½ lb. of margarine or butter. Mix in the yolk of one egg—beating well—and a tablespoonful of cinnamon powder.

Whisk the white of the egg separately, stirring this in later, and pour the whole—which should now be like a cream—into a greased mould and steam for 2½ hours. Serve with a thick, lemon-flavoured sauce.

Carrot Fritters

6 oz. cold cooked carrots	*1 tablespoonful chopped parsley*
2 tablespoonsful breadcrumbs	*1 teaspoonful chopped onion*
1 beaten egg	*½ oz. butter or margarine*
Salt and pepper to taste	*Flour as required*

Mash the carrots until smooth with the butter or margarine—in a saucepan. Stir in the onion, breadcrumbs, parsley, salt and pepper to taste, and enough of the beaten egg to bind. With floured hands, shape into small, flat cakes. Fry in fat until brown below, then turn and brown on the other side. Serve with eggs and tomato sauce.

PARSNIPS

The core of parsnips is often indigestible and tasteless. It may, therefore, be discarded if desired or, better still, fried! It is always better, from the health point of view, to cook the roots whole and to remove the skins afterwards.

Parsnips are delicious when parboiled and roasted or fried afterwards.

Boiled Parsnips

Wash the roots well, removing at the same time any diseased patches that may be seen. Cut into convenient lengths for placing in the pot, which should contain boiling water, salted in the proportion of a large tablespoonful to each $\frac{1}{2}$ gallon of water used. Boil until tender. Drain off the water, rub off the outer skin, and serve cut up into suitable portions in a warmed vegetable dish, covering with a thick white sauce.

Parsnips are particularly delicious with fish, pork, or boiled beef.

Steamed Parsnips

The vegetable should be prepared in a similar manner as above, or may be pared beforehand. It should be cut up into smaller portions and placed in the steamer. Steaming usually takes about $1\frac{1}{2}$ hours.

Mashed Parsnips

Having boiled or steamed the roots until soft, they may be mashed, mixing in a little margarine and seasoning with pepper and salt. Mashed parsnips should be served in a heated vegetable dish, garnished with a little freshly chopped parsley.

Parsnip Croquettes

3 large parsnips	*Boiling salted water*
2 tablespoonsful butter	*1 tablespoonful lemon juice*
1 beaten egg	*Flour, egg and breadcrumbs*
2 tablespoonsful cream	*Salt and pepper to taste*
1 lb. frying fat	

Wash, clean and cook the parsnips in salted boiling water until tender. Mash until perfectly smooth. There should be just over one pint of the purée. Place in a saucepan. Stir in the lemon juice and butter, over low heat. When the butter is melted, stir in the cream, egg and salt and pepper to taste. Cook until hot, stirring constantly. Remove from stove. Leave until cool, then shape into little rolls. Dip in flour, then in egg and breadcrumbs. Fry in deep, hot fat until golden. Drain on absorbent paper.

Fried Parsnip Balls

1 lb. mashed cold parsnips	1 egg
¼ lb. margarine or butter	1 tablespoonful milk
1 cupful breadcrumbs	Pepper and salt.

Mix the mashed parsnip in a saucepan with the margarine or butter and milk, and season with the pepper and salt. Heat and stir until the contents start to bubble, then add a portion of the egg, after beating well. Cool the contents and shape into balls. Roll these in eggs and breadcrumbs and fry them in boiling fat. If preferred, a batter may be used instead of the egg and breadcrumbs.

Mashed Parsnips with Carrots

For those who do not like the flavour of the parsnip alone, carrots and parsnips should be cooked separately (either boiled or steamed) and, when tender, they should be mashed with a little margarine or butter. While still warm they should be mixed together well in equal proportions and again placed in a saucepan over heat. When heated through, the mixture should be served in a warmed vegetable dish garnished with a little finely chopped parsley.

Parsnip Soup

This can be made in a similar manner to carrot soup (see p. 70). To every three or four parsnips used, it is advisable to add one tablespoonful of vinegar, together with two stems of celery and one large onion. The vinegar is added to correct the sweet flavour of the parsnips, and may be omitted for those with a sweet tooth.

Parsnip Pie

Boil or steam the parsnips, extract the cores, and mash well with a fair quantity of margarine or butter. Season with pepper and salt, and place in a greased pie dish. Garnish with some finely chopped parsley, and after dabbing with two or three pats of margarine or butter, cook in a hot oven.

Alternative pies may be made if cheese is mixed with the mashed parsnip in the proportion of about 1 to 5. A beaten egg may be added, together with some cold minced pork or beef, and minced tomatoes.

Golden Parsnips

4 medium sized parsnips	*Cayenne pepper*
3 oz. grated cheese	*Salt*
2 eggs	*Fat for frying*
5 oz. breadcrumbs	*1 tablespoonful flour*
1 oz. butter	

Boil the parsnips until tender. Drain well. Mash with the butter, pepper and salt; stir in the cheese and mix thoroughly. Form into the shape of small halved parsnips, dust with flour, then coat with egg and breadcrumbs. See that the deep fat in the pan is well heated, fry until golden brown and serve at once.

SWEDES

This vegetable can be used in the same way as, and as an alternative to, turnips. Swede soup is particularly nice.

TURNIPS

Fresh young turnips are particularly delicious, and are quite different from the coarse old roots that so many people use. Advice as to the best tender varieties to grow will be found earlier on. A young turnip does not take more than half an hour to boil, or three-quarters of an hour to steam. An old root often takes an hour to an hour and a half!

Boiled Turnips

Wash the turnips well and scrub them. Young turnips can be cooked without being pared, but old roots usually have to be pared rather thickly, as the outer skin is bitter. Place nice young roots into a saucepan of salted boiling water whole, but cut old roots up into quarters before doing so. Allow one dessertspoonful of salt to every quart of water. Boil for half an hour if young, or for three-quarters of an hour to an hour if old. Drain in a colander and serve in a warmed vegetable dish with white sauce. Season with pepper and salt.

Mashed Turnips

Take young turnips boiled or steamed whole in their skins, removing these latter if necessary when cooked, or large old roots prepared as advised for boiling, and, when thoroughly cooked, mash well, adding one or two tablespoonsful of margarine or butter. Season with pepper and salt, and serve in a mound in a warmed vegetable dish. Garnish, if required, with chopped parsley.

Turnip Cakes

Cook and mash the turnips, adding the margarine or butter as advised in the preceding recipe. Beat up one egg and mix with the turnips, together with sufficient flour to enable the mash to be made into nice round cakes. Roll these cakes in egg and breadcrumbs, or in batter, and fry a nice brown in deep fat.

Turnip Soup

6 small turnips	2 oz. margarine or butter
1 oz. flour	1 pint milk
2 pints of stock or turnip water	1 teaspoonful sugar
Salt, pepper and nutmeg to taste	

Wash and pare the turnips, cutting them up into thin slices. Put the margarine or butter into a saucepan and, when melted, add the turnips and let them cook gently for 20 minutes. Then add the two pints of stock or water and simmer for another 40 minutes.

The roots should then be taken out, rubbed through a hair-sieve, and returned to the saucepan. The milk should then be added and the soup brought to the boil. Meanwhile, mix the flour with a little milk, and when the soup comes to the boil pour in the paste and cook for another five minutes. Season with pepper and salt and a little nutmeg. Serve hot. It should be sufficient for four persons.

Turnip Salad

This is a good way of using up cold boiled turnips. They should be sliced or diced and put into a salad bowl and have a little salad dressing poured over them. The dish looks well when garnished with diced or sliced cold beetroot.

Turnips with Cheese

6 young or 4 old turnips   *3 oz. margarine or butter*
½ teacupful breadcrumbs   *½ cupful stock*
3 tablespoonsful grated cheese

Peel the turnips and boil or steam until tender. Mash well with half the margarine or butter and place in a fireproof dish, adding the stock. Season with salt and pepper and sprinkle the cheese evenly over the top. Put the remaining margarine in dabs over the surface and bake in a hot oven for a quarter of an hour or until the top browns.

Turnip Pie

4 young turnips   *1 teacupful milk*
½ teacupful breadcrumbs   *½ teacupful grated cheese*

Wash and cook the young turnips whole in boiling salted water until almost done. Take them out, peel them while hot, and cut into slices. Put these in a greased pie dish, seasoning with pepper and salt, pour on the milk, and sprinkle on the breadcrumbs and cheese. Put into a moderate oven until nicely browned.

KOHL RABI

(See p. 199).

SALSIFY

(See p. 200).

CHAPTER EIGHT

Peas and Beans

This chapter deals with the ordinary peas and beans that one expects to find in the garden or allotment.

Runner beans are very useful, for they can be made to clamber up the iron railings at the end of a garden, or to cover a shed; they can be grown up wire-netting—e.g. the tennis court surround—or up poles, which can form a good background to the harbaceous border. They are very heavy cropping, they last for a good time. They contain vitamins A, B2 and C.

Broad beans are useful, especially those that are sown in the autumn and come into use in the late spring. French beans have their place because they can be sown in May as a summer crop, and again in June and July for the autumn.

Peas, too, contain 18 per cent of carbohydrates, and from that point of view are as good as parsnips, old potatoes and salsify, and are considerably better than most other vegetables. Their calorific content per pound stands as high as 460, which is higher than that of new potatoes by 50, and almost five times as high as cauliflower or artichokes. Another advantage is that they can be sown in the autumn and then again from spring until mid-summer. The dwarf varieties will be perhaps the most useful, for they do not normally need sticks.

Another important point in favour of peas and beans is that they add nitrogen to the ground if their roots are left in after harvesting. They thus enrich the soil, and leave it in a better condition than when the seed was sown.

BROAD BEANS

The 'straw' of the broad bean is quite useful when dried, and may be used to form mats to give protection to plants in frames, or, if erected between poles, to act as windbreaks.

Soil and Manuring   The broad bean will grow on almost any soil, and no special preparation is needed. Powdery composted vegetable refuse may be added at the rate of one good barrowload per 8 sq. yds., and, in addition, 3 oz. of a good fish fertilizer per sq. yd. should be raked into the top inch.

Seed Sowing   A sowing of the Long-pod types may be made in November and January, while the Broad Windsor group should be sown during March or April. November sowings are not always successful, owing to frost or wet weather.

The rows will be 18 in. apart. The drills should be drawn out $\frac{1}{2}$ in. wide, and a row of beans should be placed in these drills so that they are 6 in. apart. The drills should be 3 in. deep.

Ten beans should be sown in a group at the ends of each row, and the plants that result may be used for filling up any gaps that appear a few weeks later.

General Cultivation   Keep a sharp look-out for the black aphis. If this appears, dust or spray with derris. It is not necessary to pinch out the tops, except with the idea of encouraging the early production of beans.

Directly the crop is over the plants should be cut down and the roots left in the ground. The tops may be rotted down for manure.

Harvesting   Pick the beans regularly when young, as this ensures a heavier crop.

Varieties

Exhibition Green Windsor: a truly green bean. Excellent flavour.

Gillett's Imperial Long-pod: large, well-filled, long pods good flavour.

Longfellow: a tall-growing variety, bearing enormous pods.

FRENCH BEANS

(Sometimes called the Dwarf or Kidney Bean)
It is useful because it comes into cropping earlier than its cousin, the runner bean, and it withstands drought better than any other vegetable crop.

Soil and Manuring   On the whole, the French bean prefers a light soil to a heavy one. The land should be prepared as advised for broad beans, only the ground where the French beans are to be grown may be cropped with lettuce first of all, and these give some protection for the young plants as they come through. The lettuce can be cut as the beans grow. This is an excellent method of inter-cropping—i.e. taking two crops from one plot of land. Add a good fish fertilizer with a 6 per cent potash content at 3–4 oz. to the sq. yd. If the soil is lacking in organic matter, give sedge peat at two bucketsful to the square yard.

Lime is necessary for all members of the pea and bean family, and may be applied to the surface of the ground after raking in the organic fertilizers, like fish, at from 4–7 oz. per sq. yd. depending on the acidity of the soil. A test must be made with a Soil Indicator or if a Fellow of the Good Gardeners Association a free soil test can be made by the Association's Soil Chemist.

Seed Sowing   It is possible to make a sowing in frames in March, and when the plants are through they can be transplanted to other frames, 8 in. square, or they may be thinned, and grown in the same frame.

Another sowing may be made early in April in a frame, but the plants which result are put outside in a sheltered border the second or third week of May. When transplanting French beans, plenty of soil should be kept around their roots.

The first sowing outside should be done during the first week of May, or even earlier in the South-West. Drills should be made 2 in. deep and ½ in. wide, and 18 in. apart. In each drill the beans should be placed 6 in. apart.

It is quite possible to sow twice as thickly as this, and to thin out in three weeks' time, transplanting the seedlings into gaps or into further rows.

The last sowing of the season should be done during the first week of July. The rows should be 18 in. apart, and the beans spaced out 8 in. apart. This spacing may be done by thinning the plants which are sown twice this thickness.

General Cultivation On rich soil the taller plants may need supporting with bushy twigs if the situation is exposed. A look-out should be kept for slugs, and these should be controlled with Draza pellets. These are blue in colour and so are not taken by the birds, I find.

Harvesting The beans should be picked when young, as regular gathering will cause an increase in the crop.

Varieties

Masterpiece: a good variety for frames and for planting out. Long handsome pods.

Processor: for sowing later. Stringless. Resistant to halo blight.

Feltham Prolific: a dwarf variety. May be planted closer than the others.

The Prince: bears heavy crops of longish pods. Almost stringless.

Pencil Pod Wax: the best yellow stringless bean.

RUNNER BEANS

As the introduction suggested, they can be grown almost anywhere where they can have an extensive root run.

Soil and Manuring It is important to start with well composted soil. Well made powdery brown compost should be applied all over the soil where the runner beans are growing at two good barrowloads to 8 sq. yds.

A fish fertilizer with a 10 per cent potash content should be raked in at 3–4 oz. to the sq. yd. a week or so before the seed is sown. Hydrated lime should be applied to the surface of the ground afterwards at, say 3 oz. per sq. yd., if the soil test shows this to be necessary.

Seed Sowing It is not generally possible to sow runner beans until early in May, and in the North until the second or third week in May. For succession, another sowing may be made early in June.

When the beans are to grow up poles, wire-netting, or string, the rows should be 5 ft. apart; but where they are to be kept cut back, and 'grown on the flat', or when the dwarf variety is grown, the rows may be 3 ft. apart.

The seed is usually sown 2 in. deep and 6 in. apart in the rows.

A number of beans are sown in a group at the end of the row, so that the seedlings may be transplanted into any blank spaces that appear when they are 3 in. or so high.

Staking The poles are usually put into position just after sowing, and may be 1 ft. apart. Double rows of poles are sometimes used, and these are joined together at the top by means of a cross pole, forming a series of inverted V's.

When it is impossible to obtain bean poles, structures should be erected consisting of wire-netting, string, and the like.

General Cultivation Runner beans that are grown on the flat should be kept 'topped' from time to time, the tops of the plants being pinched out when they are 18 in. high. This causes them to break out into further growth. A further pinching back should take place when the subsequent growths are 18 in. long. After this any further growth should be kept cut back with a pair of shears from time to time.

Slugs should be kept down by using Draza pellets, which are not liked by birds being blue in colour. If the compost is made properly and applied on top of the soil, 1 in. deep, slugs invariably disappear!

Late in June a mulch of sedge peat or rotted leaves should be put along the rows to keep in the moisture. This should be done after a heavy watering, and is particularly valuable in a dry season.

In the evening the rows may be sprayed with tepid water, as this helps the flowers to set and keeps the pods tender.

Harvesting   Picking should be done regularly to keep the plants cropping steadily and to prevent seeds developing in the pods. Surplus beans which cannot be used immediately may be kept fresh for several days if they are stood upright in water, on their stem ends.

Varieties

Hammonds Dwarf Scarlet: an early dwarf variety which never climbs, a natural dwarf kind.

3   Runner beans will remain fresh for days if placed with their stalks in a jar of water.

Crusader: a heavy cropper. Bears long, dark-green pods.
Streamline: fine flavour, long-podded, fleshy pods in
immense clusters.
White Lady: perhaps the most tender bean; the best late
variety.

WAX-POD BEAN

This is sometimes called the butter bean (but must not be
confused with the large dried white bean sold in grocers'
shops as the butter bean). It grows like the French bean, but
bears yellow pods, the whole pod being used.

Golden Wax-Pod is the best variety.

PEAS

The peas, like the beans, have nodules on their roots containing bacteria which extract nitrogen from the air. The
roots should therefore be left in the ground after harvesting.

Soil and Manuring Peas will grow on almost any soil,
providing it is limed so as to counteract acidity.

They are on the ground for only a short time, and so the
plant foods that are used should be in an available form, or
should be put on some time beforehand, so that they are in
such a form that the roots can use them when they want
them.

Composted powdery vegetable waste should be applied
on top of the soil. In addition, an organic fertilizer like fish,
or meat and bone meal should be raked in at 3 oz. to the
sq. yd.

Seed Sowing It is convenient to sow the seed in drills
which have been drawn out beforehand 2 in. wide and 3 in.
deep. In these drills the seed may be sown 2 in. apart each
way, and for the later varieties, 3 in. apart. It is never
advisable to sow peas thicker than this.

To prevent birds or mice getting the seeds, they should be soaked in a mixture of paraffin and red lead, made into the consistency of ordinary cream.

When the plants are just coming through, the rows should be protected against birds by using home-made or bought pea-guards.

Except in the North, the earliest sowings should be made in the autumn, in November and December. For such sowings it is a good plan to draw the drill out in the morning of a warm day, so as to let it dry out before actually sowing the seed in the afternoon.

A further early sowing may be made at the beginning of February or, in the North, at the beginning of March. Dwarf varieties should be chosen (round-seeded ones), the rows being 18 in. apart.

Similar varieties may be sown in pots or boxes, in frames or in the greenhouse, late in January or early in February. The plants thus raised should be put out in the border late in March or early in April.

From the beginning of April onwards, peas may be sown at regular intervals. It is quite a good plan (if there is enough room) to make another sowing directly the last row is seen above ground.

The earliest-maturing varieties may be sown again late in June or the beginning of July, so as to get good pickings in the month of September. Such sowings may follow potatoes or early cauliflowers.

The soil should be given a good flooding, if possible, and this will not only hasten the germination of the seeds, but will also give the young plants a good start.

The distance between the rows depends on the variety sown. A 3 ft. variety needs an 18 in. space between the rows, while a 4 ft. variety should have a 2 ft. space.

General Cultivation Mulches may be given along the rows as advised for runner beans. If the weather is dry, a good watering may be given from time to time in small trenches drawn out on either side of the row, rather than in the row itself.

To help the plants to climb, bushy twigs should be inserted in the ground near the peas when they are 3–4 in. high. Whenever possible, pea sticks should be used and, when these are not available, wire-netting.

Pea sticks should be placed at an angle of 45 degrees, so that the sticks on either side of the row lean inwards. The sticks in one row should be sloping at the opposite angle to the other. The wire-netting is kept upright by using bamboos.

Harvesting   Peas should be picked regularly, and no pods should be missed when ready.

Varieties

Early Onward: a heavy cropping, first early pea; 2 ft.

Duplex: a heavy cropper; bears straight pods closely packed; $2\frac{1}{2}$ ft.

Histon Mini: a prolific early variety; 12 in.

Onward: very heavy cropping; mildew resisting; $2\frac{1}{2}$ ft.

Histon Maincrop: classed as a marrowfat; $2\frac{1}{2}$ ft. Wonderful flavour.

Early Onward and Histon Mini are early varieties and may be sown in the spring and again in the autumn. Duplex and Onward may be called mid-season varieties, and Histon Maincrop treated as a main crop.

CHAPTER NINE

Pea and Bean Recipes

Peas and beans are perhaps the most popular of vegetables. Peas should never be gathered before they are actually required, and they should not be shelled until a few minutes before cooking. It is only in this way that you get the maximum food value and the maximum flavour. They are then excellent in a dish by themselves with a little dab of margarine or butter and some pepper and salt. It spoils them, I feel, to eat them with meat and another vegetable.

The same rules apply to French beans and runner beans. If they are picked hours before they are required, they get flabby and lose their flavour. When they are sliced there is no doubt that they are most digestible, but if they are picked young and only topped and tailed they are perhaps more flavoursome.

Broad beans are the richest in food value of any vegetable dealt with in this chapter. They contain vitamins, A, B and C, and are high in carbohydrate content. They are certainly a great delicacy when they are freshly picked on the young side. There is no difficulty in either boiling them or steaming them until they are tender. It is foolish to take off the outer skins of the seeds, as some housewives do, for as a result much of the flavour goes and the food value too. If desired, the skins may be removed after cooking and the 'centres' then re-cooked in a little margarine or butter. Young broad beans are delicious eaten raw with salt.

BROAD BEANS

Buttered Beans

> 1½ lb. shelled beans   1 teacupful water
> 3 oz. margarine   1 teaspoonful salt

Place the water in a saucepan and heat. Add the margarine and, when melted, put in the beans and sprinkle with salt. Bring to the boil and simmer gently for ten minutes. By then the beans will be cooked and should be served hot with the liquid after it has been thickened with a little flour.

Hotel Beans

> 1½ lb. shelled beans   1 pint water
> 1 teaspoonful salt

Place the salt in the water in a saucepan and bring to the boil. Put in the shelled beans and continue boiling until they are tender. Drain them thoroughly in a warm colander and serve in a warmed vegetable dish. Serve with a butter sauce into which a little chopped parsley has been placed.

Parsley Sauce Beans

> 1½ lb. shelled beans   ¼ pint milk
> 2 tablespoonsful chopped parsley   1 pinch mixed herbs
> 1 teaspoonful granulated sugar   ½ pint stock
> 1 egg   Pepper and salt to season

Cook the beans, as in the preceding recipe, until nearly done. Then drain them in a colander and place them in a pan with the herbs, the sugar, and the stock. Cook until tender, and then beat up the egg in the milk and pour this on to the beans. Continue to heat until thoroughly hot. Serve with the finely chopped parsley sprinkled evenly over the top.

Beans Ordinaire

> 1½ lb. shelled beans   1 oz. margarine or butter
> 1 pint water   Pepper and salt to taste
> 1 teaspoonful salt

Bring the salted water to the boil. Place in the beans and boil for a quarter of an hour or more, until tender. When properly cooked, drain through a colander, returning the beans to the saucepan together with the margarine or butter and the pepper and salt. Shake over heat until the fat melts and the beans get really hot. Serve in a warmed vegetable dish.

Broad Beans Creamed

This is a method of using up old beans that need to be disguised a little before serving. Boil the beans well and pass through a wire sieve to form a purée. Before sieving them strain off most of the water to prevent the finished mixture from being too thin. Serve on pieces of very hot buttered toast, and garnish with grated cheese or some very finely minced cold beef.

Broad Bean Soup

1 lb. shelled beans	*1 teaspoonful chopped parlsey*
3 pints water	*1 dessertspoonful flour*
1 good slice bacon	*1 oz. butter*
1 dessertspoonful finely chopped onion	*Salt, pepper, sugar*

Boil beans in salted water for ten minutes. Remove skins. Fry together in a pan the onion, parsley, and bacon. When brown, add stock and boil together with the beans. Cook gently until beans are tender, and then sieve through a coarse wire sieve. Place in saucepan and thicken with flour previously mixed with a little stock. Season to taste and add sugar. Serve very hot with small pieces of toast.

Bean Salad

Fresh young broad beans may be used alone as a salad, sprinkled with a little salt, or may be mixed in with other vegetables in a lettuce salad. Cold cooked broad beans can also be used in a vegetable salad as desired.

Bacon and Beans

¼ lb. bacon	2 oz. margarine or butter
2 oz. flour	2 lb. beans
½ pint stock	Pepper and salt

Cook the bacon until pale brown, and then cut into small pieces, dip in flour, and fry in margarine or butter until quite cooked. Add the stock and boil all together. Cook gently after putting in the beans, which have already been cooked. Season to taste with salt and pepper, sprinkle with chopped ham, and simmer for twenty minutes. Be careful when stirring not to break the beans. Serve in the centre of a very hot dish surrounded by triangles of toast.

FRENCH BEANS

French beans should not be gathered for any length of time before they are cooked, as this causes them to lose much of their delicious flavour and a great deal of their goodness.

A very good way to cook them is to top and tail them and steam them in a small amount of margarine or butter. The length of time needed to steam them is determined by their age and size. Some people prefer to boil them in salted water and, when drained and put in a hot vegetable dish, to pour some melted butter or margarine over them.

Boiled French Beans

Cut off the heads and tails and a very thin strip down the sides of the beans. Cut the remainder into strips slantwise down the bean. Drop into cold water until needed. Put into a saucepan of boiling salted water. Do not put a lid on the saucepan, and boil very rapidly for twenty minutes. Drain well and serve in a hot vegetable dish with a little melted butter or margarine if desired.

Sauté French Beans

Boil the beans until tender. Drain and fry in a basket in deep fat until the beans are lightly brown. Season to taste with salt and pepper.

Tomato and Bean Salad

Allow half the quantity of tomatoes to that of French beans. Cook the beans and, when cold, cut into short pieces and mix with sliced tomatoes. Pour over this a dressing made of 2 parts oil, 1 part vinegar, and pepper and salt to taste.

Onion and Bean Salad

½ pint cooked sliced beans *1 medium-sized onion*
1 dessertspoonful dripping *¼ pint stock*
1 tablespoonful white vinegar *Salt, pepper, paprika*

Stir the beans into the heated dripping, then add the vinegar, salt, pepper, and paprika. Lastly mix in the very finely chopped onion. Heat the stock. Stir in all the ingredients and leave to cool. Serve with cold ham.

French Beans with Anchovies or Herrings

2 oz. butter or margarine *½ small onion*
1 pint cooked beans   *1 tin anchovies or herrings*

Fry the beans in the heated butter or margarine until brown. Place in the centre of a heated meat dish and sprinkle with chopped parsley. Place the anchovies or herrings round the beans and serve.

Savoury Beans

1 pint cooked beans *2 eggcupsful lemon juice*
2 oz. margarine   *Pinch of cinnamon*

Thoroughly heat the beans in the melted margarine or butter. Mix in the cinnamon and lemon juice. Serve on pieces of hot buttered toast.

RUNNER BEANS

Boiled Runner Beans

When young, runner beans may be cooked whole. Just take off the 'tops and tails', and boil them in water to which some salt has been added. When they are older they should be 'stringed' and cut up into slices.

Runner Bean Salad

Runner beans when cut up into thin slices, make an excellent addition to a salad.

See French Beans for other recipes suitable for runner beans.

WAX-POD BEANS

These beans may be used in exactly the same way as French or runner beans.

PEAS

Peas, like many other summer vegetables, must be picked just when they are ready for use to appreciate their flavour to the full. They should be gathered just before they are needed for cooking, as, if they are kept after being shelled, they are apt to become a little hard.

Boiled Peas

One of the most important things about cooking peas is to cook them in as little water as is absolutely necessary. They should be just covered with boiling salted water to which a few small sprigs of mint have been added. Young peas should not be boiled for more than fifteen minutes, or they will split. Drain off the water and serve in a hot vegetable dish.

Buttered Peas

1 pint shelled peas	*1 teaspoonful salt*
1 teaspoonful sugar	*1½ oz. margarine or butter*
2 sprigs mint	*1 quart water*

Put the peas into quickly boiling water which has previously been seasoned with salt and sugar, and add the mint. Boil quickly, without the lid on the pan, for fifteen minutes. If peas are older, longer time must be allowed for boiling. Drain and remove the mint, then put the peas into a vegetable dish. Pour the melted margarine or butter over them, and sprinkle with a little pepper.

French Peas

1 pint shelled peas	*2 sprigs mint*
2 oz. margarine or butter	*Pepper and salt*
1 tablespoonful chopped parsley	

Cook the peas in rapidly boiling water. Add the salt and the mint and, as before, keep the pan uncovered for fifteen to twenty minutes, according to age. Drain well and shake the saucepan until they are quite dry; then add the butter or margarine, parsley, and season with pepper. Stir over a low heat for a few seconds. Serve while very hot.

Hors d'Oeuvre

2 large cooked new potatoes	*1 small beetroot (boiled)*
½ pint cooked peas	*Salad dressing or mayonnaise*
1 hard-boiled egg	*Parsley*

Cut all the ingredients, with the exception of the peas and the yolk of the hard-boiled egg, into dice. Mix with the peas and the salad dressing or mayonnaise. Put on small individual dishes or one large dish, and garnish with parsley and the sieved yolk of egg.

Pod Soup

Look over the pods and throw away all those that are blemished. Wash the remainder well and place in an aluminium saucepan with sufficient water to cover them well. Boil until the pods are quite tender and most of the water has been absorbed. Rub through a fine hair sieve until nothing but the strings remain. Replace the purée in a saucepan and season to taste. Serve very hot with strips of toast.

Pea Soup (i)

1 pint stock	*2 sprigs mint*
1 pint shelled peas	*Small dessertspoonful flour*
2 oz. margarine or butter	*Pepper and salt*

Place a little of the butter or margarine into a steamer, add the peas and the mint, and steam with the cover on for twenty minutes to half an hour. Add the stock and water and boil in a saucepan until tender. Strain, and pass the vegetables through a sieve. Melt the remainder of the margarine or butter in another pan, sprinkle in the flour, and mix to a cream. Add the purée and stir until boiling. Season to taste and serve with triangles of toast.

Pea Soup (ii)

3 large peeled potatoes	*1 pint boiling water*
½ lb. shelled peas	*2 oz. margarine or butter*
2 medium-sized onions	*Pepper and salt*

Cut the vegettable into small pieces, put them into boiling water and bring to the boil. Add the peas and boil gently all together for half an hour. Put the mixture through a fine sieve, return to the pan, and bring to the boil, adding the butter or margarine just before serving. Stir it in well and serve very hot.

Cucumber and Pea Salad

Cut the cucumber into dice of about 1 in. square. Place in rings on a large meat dish, and into the centres of the rings put heaps of cooked green peas. Over this pour a mayonnaise dressing and garnish with dice of cooked beetroot.

Pea 'Shape'

½ lb. cooked peas
1 oz. margarine or butter
1 small spoonful castor sugar
3 tomatoes

1 dessertspoonful flour
2 tablespoonsful milk
Pepper and salt

Boil the peas in salted and sugared water until quite tender, and drain thoroughly. Rub through a fine sieve. Put the pulp in a saucepan with the margarine or butter. Mix the flour, milk, pepper and salt to a smooth cream. Add to the pulp and mix until thickened over a low heat. Place heaped up in the centre of a meat dish, putting round the edge, tomatoes cut in thin slices.

Bacon and Peas

1 pint shelled peas
1 medium-sized onion
2 oz. margarine or butter
1 oz. flour

2 sprigs mint
¼ lb. bacon
1 teaspoonful salt
1 pint water

Boil the peas until tender, with the mint, and strain. Chop the onion and cook also until quite soft. Put on one side. Cut the bacon into strips and fry. Brown the onions in the fat that is left. Mix the margarine or butter and flour into a cream and into this put the peas and the bacon. Mix all together in a saucepan over a low heat. Serve on a hot dish, garnished with toast.

Pea Balls

1 pint shelled peas
1 small onion (shredded)
1 breakfastcupful cooked
  minced beef

1 egg
2 oz. margarine or butter
Breadcrumbs

Boil the peas in salted water together with onion shredded very finely. Rub through a sieve. Mix with breadcrumbs, sufficient to absorb the moisture, and mix all together with the minced beef. Melt the margarine or butter and pour into the mixture to help to bind it. Shape into balls, coat with egg and breadcrumbs, and fry until a golden brown in deep fat. Serve on a large meat dish garnished with finely chopped parsley.

Iced Mould made with Peas

1 pint cooked peas	*1 plain jelly*
½ pint milk	*1 oz. sugar*

Rub the peas through a fine sieve and place in a mixing bowl. Melt the jelly in sufficient water to cover it. Add the sugar to this when melted, and last of all add the peas and milk. Pour into a wet mould and leave to set. This is an excellent sweet for those who prefer something 'not quite so sweet'.

Savoury Pea Shapes

½ pint sieved cooked peas	*½ onion*
1 egg	*1 oz. margarine or butter*
1 dessertspoonful milk	

Mix well together the sieved peas, milk and very finely grated onion. Bind with a well-beaten egg and the melted margarine or butter. When thoroughly mixed, place in greased moulds and bake in a moderate oven until set. Turn out on a heated meat dish and surround with well-browned chipped potatoes. Serve very hot.

CHAPTER TEN

Growing Potatoes

The potato is certainly an important crop to grow, but it is more cheaply grown on a large scale with tractors and ploughs than it is in the private garden. Transport, however, is always an important factor, and so it may be necessary to grow some potatoes in and near all towns.

Not only are more potatoes eaten than any other vegetable, but they are an excellent cleaning crop. New potatoes are more valuable than old potatoes, and are also richer in vitamins. It is therefore suggested that the householder should concentrate on early- and mid-season varieties if he has a garden or allotment of limited size.

Soil Potatoes can be grown on all soils, though some produce tubers of an inferior flavour to others. It is said that the heavy clays and peaty soils produce waxy tubers. Badly drained or low-lying land should be avoided, although even such a situation may be productive of good and sound crops if the summer is hot and dry. Situations which are confined or overhung by large trees are also unsuitable.

The best potatoes are grown in an open, sunny situation on a well-drained, medium soil—not a pure clay or too light a sand. A clay can be made friable, but it is difficult to work during wet periods, and so is a 'nuisance' during harvesting and planting times.

Preparation of the Soil   One of the best ways of preparing the soil for potatoes is by rotovation with a mechanical rotovator, and this should be done shallowly in the spring. The alternative to rotovation is a light forking.

Manuring   The land can be manured in the spring with powdery composted vegetable refuse over the rows at planting time. In addition a compounded fish manure with 6 per cent potash content should be applied at 3 oz. to the square yard.

It is most important to buy seed either of Scottish or Irish origin. Tubers should be taken from plants free from virus diseases. With any seed purchased, the gardener should obtain the Ministry's certificate number. This is his guarantee.

The tubers used for seed should be about the size of a hen's egg, and should weigh about 2 oz. Gardeners who obtain larger tubers should cut these in two in such a way that each portion contains the necessary 'eyes'. This cutting should take place just before the tubers are planted. If done earlier, some loss of crop results.

If the potatoes are bought early in the year (and this is a good plan), they should be boxed up—that is to say, placed in shallow trays to sprout, rose end upwards. (The rose end is the end where most of the eyes are found, and is the opposite end to that which was attached to the underground stem.) 'Sprouting' ensures an earlier and heavier yield.

The market gardener uses a potato tray, 2 ft. 6 in. long, 1 ft. 6 in. wide, and $3\frac{1}{2}$ in. deep. In the corners there are small square posts standing 3 in. above the sides. These posts are there so that the trays may be stood one above the other, while the sprouting process is going on, i.e. without injuring the sprout.

These trays containing the potatoes should then be stacked in a cool, light, airy place where there is no possibility of their being frozen. Some gardeners use cold greenhouses, while others find a loft or a shed quite convenient. Air should circulate freely amongst the trays, and pathways should be left so that potatoes may be looked over occasionally to remove those that are going rotten.

When the tubers start to grow they should be disbudded, leaving only the two strongest shoots at the rose end of the tubers. When the time comes for planting, the trays should be taken into the garden. The tubers should then be taken out one at a time and placed carefully in the bottom of a shallow drill without breaking off the sprouts. If planting is done carelessly, the sprouts will break off easily and all the trouble spent on them in the trays will be wasted.

The object of sprouting the seed is to secure a few weeks' growth before planting takes place. Sprouted potatoes are therefore ready to lift several weeks earlier than potatoes planted unsprouted. This saving of time also ensures heavier crops as the potatoes have, in consequence, a longer season of growth.

Planting   The earliest potatoes should be planted in shallow drills made in the compost covered soil about 2 in. deep, the tubers being planted 12 in. apart in the rows. For this earliest planting the tubers should be harvested when they are quite small.

The drills for ordinary early potatoes should be 1 ft. 9 in. apart, the seed being placed 12 in. apart in the rows. The ridges which can be made with compost for the second earlies should be 2 ft. 3 in. apart, the seed being 1 ft. 3 in. apart in the rows. For the main crops the rows should be 2 ft. 6 in. apart and the tubers 1 ft. 6 in. apart in the rows.

No seed potatoes should be planted deeper than 2 in. and with the earliest varieties, 1 in. will do. The rows should run North and South and, after planting, plenty of compost should be placed over the rows so as to leave a slight ridge.

Planting should take place in the South about the third week of March, and in the North as late as the second week of April. Though it sounds peculiar to say so, it is better to plant the late potatoes first, and the early potatoes last. The lates have a longer season of growth and are not through the ground soon enough to be affected by a late spring frost.

Some compost gardeners in fact put the seed tubers on top

4   Seed potatoes are placed on trays to sprout with the rose end, containing most eyes, uppermost. At planting time the potatoes should have sturdy shoots about an inch long, and are planted shallowly, being careful not to knock off the shoots.

of the ground and then cover them with old, partially rotted straw 9 in. or so deep or they use good compost instead. The potatoes then grow through the straw or compost.

General Cultivation   Directly the foliage appears through the compost, gardeners should see that the tubers are fully covered and more compost may be added if necessary—then, if there is any fear of frost, the tops may be covered with a length of sacking which may be removed when fear of frost is past.

When the tops are half-grown it may be necessary to add a little more compost or sedge peat on either side. At this time the stems of the plant should be about 8 in. high.

Further additions are only necessary if the tubers appear to peep through the compost—the idea being to prevent the potatoes from greening.

A sharp look-out should be kept for the potato blight from June onwards, and directly there is any sign of the disease, the leaves and stems should be given a thorough spraying with a Bordeaux mixture, or a dusting with a copper-lime dust.

The Flat System   Planting on the flat can be done on light land which is apt to dry out quickly if raised into ridges. The land should be well manured and brought into a good tilth. At planting time, shallow holes are dug along a line marked out, one for each potato, which another person following behind places in the hole. The soil from the second row of holes is used to cover up those in the first row, and so on to the end of the plot. An active man and his pal can in this manner plant half an acre of potatoes in four hours.

The Lazy-Bed System   This system is useful on soil where the water level is near the surface. It consists of making beds 4–5 ft. wide, with deep trenches between, which drain away the superfluous moisture. The seed tubers are placed on the surface, one row at each side of the bed. Soil is taken from between the beds to cover the seed and again to earth up the plants, and in this way the trenches are formed.

To Dig Potatoes in Mid-June   Good seed should be purchased, which should be sprouted, as previously advised. A piece of ground should be selected in a sheltered position and which is inclined to the South or South-West. This should be lightly forked up, and thoroughly composted vegetable refuse added.

In mid-February the ground should be got up into ridges,

6 in. high and 18 in. apart. In March, 2 in. of compost should be laid in the bottom of each ridge. The sprouted sets should be laid on this, 10 in. apart, and be covered with 2 in. more of the compost. The ridges should then be made trim by drawing the soil from the sides over the compost. As the tops begin to show, and if it threatens to be frosty at night time, some dry straw or bracken should be placed over the rows. This should be removed each morning. It is easier to give protection against frost by the use of sacking.

By this system a good crop should be harvested at the end of the second week of June.

Lifting and Storing   The rows of early potatoes may be lifted as soon as the tubers are of a suitable size. The lifting should be done on a fine day, if possible, and the potatoes will come out clean and bright and look far more attractive.

The main crop need not be lifted to be stored until the haulm has died down. If, however, the haulm is diseased, it should be cut off and composted, as if it is allowed to die down naturally it may cause the crop to rot. The heat engendered in the compost heap kills all the disease spores.

The early and second-early potatoes will be dug up and used as desired. The main crops will be harvested and be stored in clamps (or hogs, pies, or hales, as they are called in various districts). When the tubers are coated with soil, this should be rubbed off with the hands before clamping.

The ground on which the clamp is to stand should, if possible, be higher than the general level. In no case should it be lower.

Before clamping, the potatoes should be fairly dry and any showing traces of disease should be removed and used immediately.

The tubers should be piled up in a long, ridge-shaped heap about 3½ ft. high and 3 ft. wide. They should then be covered with straw or bracken or other dry litter, to a depth of about 6 in., and over the straw a 6 in. covering of soil should be placed neatly. Don't cover with the soil for fourteen days, however, so as to allow the tubers to sweat.

The surface should be made smooth and firm with the spade, so that the rain will run off. The soil for covering should be taken from the ground outside the clamp, and during this operation a trench is cut all round to carry away the water and so keep the contents dry. Ventilating holes should be cut through the top of the ridge about 6 ft. apart, and a tuft of straw pulled through each hole and allowed to project. These tufts should be twisted.

If there is enough room in a sound, dry shed, potatoes may be stored there instead of being clamped. A good thickness of straw should be put between the potatoes and the outside walls, and they should be well covered over the top to protect them from frost and to exclude light.

Varieties

Earlies

Ninety-fold: the earliest potato, apt to be soapy.

Arran Pilot: a popular early; kidney-shaped.

Home Guard: a heavy cropper; large, fine shaped tubers with shallow eyes.

Sharpes Express: a white kidney; good quality; keeps well.

Second Earlies

Arran Comrade: a round variety, of excellent cooking quality.

Red Craigs Royal: bears large oval tubers of excellent quality.

Great Scot: often grown as a main crop; one of the best-known white round potatoes.

Arran Banner: a very heavy cropper; tubers are white, round and somewhat flat. Is immune.

Main Crops

Arran Victory: a round, main crop with a bright purple skin.

Gladstone: a variety resembling King Edward, but immune to wart disease. Produces a heavy crop of even-sized tubers.

Kerr's Pink: a coloured, round, heavy yielder of good quality.

Dr. Macintosh: a white kidney; shallow eyes; excellent skin; moderate-sized tubers.

King Edward (Para crinkle-free): a coloured kidney; very popular, very delicious.

Majestic: an immune variety; a heavy cropper and good keeper; a white kidney.

Special Note: The use of the word 'immune' means immune to wart disease, and not immune to all diseases. Under the Ministry of Agriculture's regulations, those who have land subject to this disease must grow immune varieties only.

CHAPTER ELEVEN

Potato Recipes

The potato is undoubtedly the most popular vegetable in the country. It is almost impossible these days for a housewife to cater without potatoes. Not only is it one of the simplest vegetables to grow in the garden, but it is also one of the cheapest to produce.

Potatoes are a good source of vitamins B and C, and contain a certain amount of vitamin A. They provide the body with heat and energy; they also contain much ash and salt, and are an excellent anti-scorbutic.

Despite the fact that it has been said again and again that the health-giving qualities of the tubers lie just under the skin, people insist on peeling before cooking. To conserve the protein and mineral matter, a potato should be steamed, boiled or baked in its jacket. Where peeling is absolutely essential, it should be done as thinly as possible.

The advantage of growing potatoes in the garden is that the sooner the new potatoes are cooked and eaten after they are harvested, the better do they taste. The gardener should avoid growing the potatoes with deep eyes and knobs.

Brief Potato Hints

1. To prevent potatoes freezing in store, stand a pail of water alongside.

2. Potatoes for dicing: 1 lb. yields 2½ large teacups.
3. Potatoes for mashing: 1 lb. yields 2¼ large teacups.
4. The allowance of potatoes per week per head should be: man, 5–7 lb.; woman, 3–4 lb.; young boy, 4–6 lb.; young girl, 3–4 lb.; child 3–5 years, 2 lb.

Boiled Potatoes

(i) Peeled
Peel thinly, putting them into cold water when pared. Place in saucepan, using a quart of water and 1 teaspoonful of salt per pound of potatoes. Bring to the boil and simmer for twenty to thirty minutes. Drain, cover with lid, stand for a few minutes, and then place in a warmed vegetable dish.

(ii) With their Skins
Wash and scrub potatoes. Place in saucepan, using same water per weight as above. Boil for thirty minutes. Test with fork; when soft, drain off water, replace lid, and stand for 2–3 minutes. Serve either peeled or unpeeled.

New Potatoes

Get the potatoes straight from the garden, wash and scrape, and put them with a good sprig of mint into boiling water, plus a teaspoonful of salt to a quart of water. Boil until tender. Pour away water, allow to stand, with lid of saucepan partly removed, until dry. Serve in hot vegetable dish with a little melted butter or margarine and chopped parsley.

Steamed Potatoes

Prepare as for boiled potatoes, sprinkle with salt, and place in steamer. Steam for forty to sixty minutes until tender. Finish off as for boiled potatoes.

N.B. It is always better to steam old potatoes, as this prevents their falling to pieces.

Baked Potatoes

Choose even-sized potatoes. Wash, scrub and prick over with fork. Place in moderate oven (temperature 350°F) for about an hour. Turn potatoes twice while baking. Do not allow them to touch each other in the oven. Serve in open dish, otherwise they become sodden.

Roast Potatoes

Prepare potatoes as for boiling. Cut up into even sizes. Dry in a clean cloth and place in the boiling fat around the roast $1\frac{1}{4}$ hours before the meat is cooked. Baste occasionally. Remove joint and put on hot dish with cover to keep warm. Leave potatoes in dish, putting this into the hot part of the oven to brown. If gas-oven, turn gas up higher.

Chipped Potatoes

Wash and peel old potatoes. Cut into uniform strips $\frac{1}{4}$ in. thick and $\frac{1}{4}$ in. broad. Throw these into cold water when cut. When ready, dry well with a clean cloth. Place plenty of fat in a deep frying pan and heat. Place chips in gradually, to avoid cooling the fat. Fry until golden brown and drain. If in frying basket, sprinkle with salt and pepper and shake. Serve in hot vegetable dish.

Baked Mashed Potatoes

$1\frac{1}{2}$ lb. mashed potatoes	Salt, pepper and paprika
$\frac{1}{2}$ pint cream	to taste

Season the potatoes with salt, pepper and a little paprika to taste. Pack into a shallow buttered fireproof dish. Beat the cream until stiff. Pile on top of potato. Sprinkle lightly with paprika. Bake in a moderate oven until piping hot. This makes an extremely attractive addition to any kind of meat.

Stuffed Potatoes

Bake large potatoes in their skins. When ready cut each in

half with a sharp knife and scoop out the inside without breaking the skin. Place this 'inside' in a bowl and whisk with a fork, adding small pats of margarine or butter from time to time, and a little milk. When frothy, place in saucepan to heat, adding a well-beaten egg and some grated cheese. Replace mixture in skins, put back into oven to reheat, and brown. Serve hot, garnished with parsley.

N.B. If preferred the potatoes may be stuffed with tomato, cooked minced meat, chopped ham, or chopped fried mushrooms.

Potato Balls

Boil potatoes and mash them. Season with pepper and salt and add a little chopped parsley and a knob of margarine or butter. Mix well, adding one well-beaten egg. Shape into balls, cover with egg and breadcrumbs, and fry as for chipped potatoes. Usually takes ten minutes.

Devonshire Potatoes

(Another good way of using up mashed potatoes.) Put a little fat into a frying pan so that when melted it covers the whole of the bottom. Melt this fat, spread mashed potatoes evenly over pan to a depth of 1 in. or so. Leave on the top of a hot stove or very low gas until the bottom is deep brown all over. Turn out on a flat, warm dish so that the brown side is uppermost.

Potato Salad

Boil or steam waxy potatoes until they are cooked and still firm. While hot, cut up into small dice of an even size. Put into a basin, stir in mayonnaise, season with salt and pepper, being careful not to break the potato. Serve in salad bowl sprinkled with chopped parsley.

N.B. For Mayonnaise Sauce see p. 180.

This salad can be varied by adding chopped onion, chopped tomato, chopped fresh celery, etc.

Potato and Onion Salad

18 spring onions	*2 lb. potatoes*
24 radishes	*1 cupful mint sauce*
2 lettuce	*½ teaspoonful finely chopped mint*
1 handful each of mustard and cress	

Boil the potatoes, drain, mash until smooth with a spoonful of butter and some hot milk. Sprinkle with chopped mint and beat well into the potato. Divide into six portions and place one on each plate, making it into a small mound and decorate with shredded lettuce, the chopped onions, cress and mustard mixed, and the radishes halved. Make the mint sauce with a little extra sugar and serve in a tureen.

Potato Cream Soup

1 cup mashed boiled potatoes	*1 dessertspoonful flour*
1 cup potato water	*1 small onion*
1½ cups hot milk	*1 teaspoonful minced parsley*
1 teaspoonful butter or margarine	*Pepper and salt*

Place the potatoes in saucepan, adding onion, chopped finely, and parsley. Pour on potato water. Bring to boil and simmer for twenty minutes. In another pan melt butter or margarine. Stir in flour gradually. When paste, add hot milk by degrees. Stir until boiling. To this add contents of other saucepan. Salt and pepper to taste. Sufficient for three persons.

Potato Ribbons

Choose large potatoes, well shaped and smooth. Peel, wash, then wipe dry before cutting them round and round like peeling apples. Use a sharp knife and keep the ribbons, if possible, of even thickness. Put in a pan of hot fat deep enough to cover them; fry until golden brown, drain; and season with pepper and salt. They should be crisp and unbroken when served in a very hot dish.

Potato and Onion Roll

1 lb. potatoes
2 eggs
2 tablespoonsful herbs
3 tablespoonsful breadcrumbs

1 lb. onions
3 oz. butter or margarine
Salt and Pepper

Parboil the onions. Drain them, chop finely, then add potatoes boiled and mashed. Rub in the butter or margarine. Season with herbs, pepper and salt. Add one well-beaten egg and form the mixture into a long sausage-like roll. Brush over with the other egg (beaten well). Roll in the breadcrumbs. Place on a buttered tin and bake for twenty minutes.

Potato and Leek Soup

6 medium-sized leeks
2 pints water
6 medium-sized potatoes

1 dessertspoonful butter or margarine
Pepper and salt

Wash, trim, and chop up leeks. Peel, prepare, and cut up potatoes. Put into saucepan, cover with water, and bring to the boil. Simmer for two hours. Add butter or margarine. Add pepper and salt to taste, and, to improve appearance, stir in a little milk just before serving. Sufficient for three or four persons.

Scottish Potato Soup

½ lb. neck of mutton
6 large potatoes
1 large carrot

2 onions
Stock or water

Place mutton in saucepan, cover with two quarts of stock or water; add onions chopped up finely. Grate carrot, cut up potatoes into small pieces, add to saucepan, simmer for two hours. When cooked, rub through sieve and, if desired, add a little milk. Sufficient for five persons.

Potatoes are invaluable with fish. Everybody knows about fish and chips! They are first class for making fish balls, fish hotpot, fish pie, etc.

Fish and Potato Pie

2 cupsful mashed or diced boiled potatoes	1 cupful boiled peas
1 cupful cooked fish	1 cup white sauce
1 teaspoonful chopped onion	Pepper and salt

Melt a little butter or margarine in a frying pan. Place over a low heat and stir in the onion until it turns clear. Then add the white sauce, and stir in the cooked potato and fish, having seasoned with pepper and salt. Put half the mixture in a greased fireproof dish and place the peas on top. Cover with the rest of the mixture and bake in a moderate oven until pale brown. If preferred, serve with green salad. Sufficient for four persons.

Salmon Pie

Mash the fish well and place a layer in a greased dish. Cover with mashed potatoes and place a layer of finely chopped onions on top. Repeat this process until the dish is nearly full, then cover the whole with a thick layer of white sauce. Bake in a moderate oven for about an hour.

Hotpot—Fish and Potato

1 lb. white fish	1 small tablespoonful flour
1 onion	1 tablespoonful margarine
½ lb. tomatoes	or butter
½ pint of the fish stock	Flour, pepper and salt
¾ lb. sliced potatoes	

Boil the fish for ten minutes in a little water. Grease the bottom of a fireproof dish and place on the bottom a layer of the sliced potato and onion. On this place the boneless parboiled fish. Sprinkle with some flour and some salt and pepper. Then cover with the tomato, neatly sliced, flour, pepper and salt again, and lay in the remainder of the onion and potatoes. After covering, cook in a moderate oven for fifty minutes. Sufficient for four persons.

Potato Omelette

5 medium-sized potatoes	½ cupful milk
4 eggs	1 dessertspoonful flour
1 oz. breadcrumbs	Pepper and salt
1½ oz. margarine or butter	

Boil the potatoes, dry them well afterwards, and mash with half the margarine or butter, adding the breadcrumbs. Add the eggs, sprinkle with pepper and salt and a dessertspoonful of flour. Whisk well. Place the remaining margarine or butter in the pan and when hot pour in the mixture. Fry over a moderate heat until golden brown. Serve hot. Sufficient for four persons.

Potato Cheese

1 lb. boiled potatoes	1 oz. dripping
¼ pint milk	Pepper and salt
1½ oz. grated cheese	

Mash the potatoes while still warm, adding the milk gradually and half the quantity of grated cheese. Grease a small pie dish well, place the mixture in position, smooth, and sprinkle with the rest of the grated cheese. Put one or two dabs of the dripping on the top and bake in a hot oven. Serve hot. Sufficient for two persons.

Potato Pie

½ lb. cold meat (minced)	½ pint stock
1 lb. mashed potatoes	2 tablespoonsful flour
3 tablespoonsful hot dripping	1 teaspoonful baking powder
½ lb. cooked vegetables (any)	Pepper and salt

Make the crust by mixing the mashed potatoes with the flour, baking powder, and the hot dripping, and season with salt and pepper. Roll this out lightly, and with half of it line a greased pie dish. Fill in with the minced cold meat and chopped-up cooked vegetables and add what seasoning is desired. Thicken the stock with a little flour and pour on.

Cover over with the remainder of the crust. Bake in a moderate oven for an hour. Serve hot. Sufficient for four persons.

Cottage Pie

1 lb. steamed mashed potatoes	*2 oz. margarine or butter*
1 lb. cold minced meat	*½ pint water or stock*
2 tablespoonsful flour	*if available*
1 finely chopped onion	

Fry the chopped onion until pale brown with a little of the margarine or butter. Then stir in the flour gradually, adding the water or the stock by degrees at the same time. Season with pepper and salt and keep stirring over a low heat until thick. Then add the minced meat, stirring for another 3–4 minutes. Grease a pie dish, put in the warm meat, smooth, and cover with the mashed potatoes. These will be improved if they are first of all mixed with a little margarine or butter and milk. Spread this neatly and prick over with a fork. Bake in a hot oven. Sufficient for four persons.

Potato Cakes

1 lb. mashed potatoes	*Baking powder*
4 oz. flour	*Pinch of salt*
3 oz. dripping or margarine	

Mix potatoes and flour well together, mix in dripping, and add the salt and baking powder. This should be mixed with water to a stiff dough and rolled out to about a quarter of an inch thickness. Cut into rounds and bake quickly in a hot oven until golden brown. Serve very hot with butter.

Potato Apple Cake

1½ lb. cooked potatoes	*5 oz. flour*
1 teaspoonful salt	*1½ oz. melted margarine or butter*
3 medium-sized apples	

Use the potatoes while they are still hot. Mash them carefully with a little margarine or butter. Place on a board and

5 Cooking a potato and apple cake.

sprinkle with salt. Add the melted fat and knead in enough flour to make a soft, pliable dough. Care should be taken not to add too much flour. Roll out and divide into two cakes. On one piece put a layer of three medium-sized apples, sliced—place the other piece round on top and pinch the edges together. Bake in a moderate oven. When cooked, split the cake open, turn the top back, and put small pieces of butter or margarine on the top, together with some sugar. Then put the top back and return the cake to the oven until the sugar and butter are melted.

Potato and Lentil Purée

½ lb. potatoes	½ oz. dripping
4 oz. lentils	A few bacon rinds
1 small onion	3 pints vegetable water
2 carrots	3 level teaspoonsful salt
Few mutton bones, if available	¼ level teaspoonful pepper

Soak the lentils overnight. Chop the onion finely and fry with the bacon rinds and dripping for five minutes. Peel and grate potatoes and carrots on a coarse grater and add to the onion, together with the vegetable water, lentils, seasoning and bones. Cover the pan and simmer gently for 1½ hours. Mash well or rub through a sieve, after removing the bones and bacon rinds, and then reheat the mixture and serve immediately.

Potato Sweet Pudding

2 lb. boiled potatoes
3 oz. margarine or butter
1 small cupful hot milk
Sugar to taste

2 eggs
Juice and rind of 1 lemon
Pinch of salt

Mash the potatoes smoothly. Mix in the sugar, hot milk, and margarine or butter; also the rind and juice of the lemon, and the salt. Well beat the egg yolks, and add these. Lastly, whisk the whites thoroughly and add to the mixture. Put into a greased baking dish and bake for forty minutes. Serve very hot. The addition of a little jam or treacle sauce is an improvement. Sufficient for four persons.

Savoury Potato Pudding

3 lb. boiled potatoes
¼ lb. grated cheese
¼ lb. shredded beef suet

1 teacupful milk
Pepper, salt, nutmeg

Mash the potatoes and add the suet and other ingredients. Put the mixture into a well greased dish and bake in a hot oven for about half an hour. This may be varied by the addition of cooked flaked haddock, shelled shrimps etc., stirred into the mixture, which will give increased flavour. Sufficient for six persons.

Potato Flan

1 lb. cooked potatoes
1 onion
1 tablespoonful finely
    chopped parsley
3 oz. minced pork

4 tablespoonsful flour
2 eggs
¼ pint milk
4 oz. margarine or butter

Use ½ lb. of potatoes and 4 oz. of the flour to make the potato pastry. Season to taste. Line a flan case with this. For the filling: fry the onion (sliced) and the pork for three minutes, and then spread this mixture over the pastry case.

Beat the eggs with the remaining potatoes and season to taste. Add the parsley and mix in the milk. The mixture should be slack enough to pour; if not, add a little more milk. Bake in a moderate oven for about three-quarters of an hour.

Potato Bread

½ cup mashed potatoes	1 tablespoonful butter or margarine
1 cup potato water	1 yeast or dough cake or ½ oz. yeast
2 teaspoonsful castor sugar	¼ cup tepid water
1 lb. flour	¾ teaspoonful salt

Scald the liquids and stir in the salt, sugar and butter or margarine. Cool until tepid. Add the yeast cake, having softened it in tepid water. When thoroughly dissolved, stir in half the flour and the well mashed potatoes. Then work in the remainder of the flour and make a smooth, elastic dough. Cover and stand in a warm temperature (71–82°F). Leave until risen to double the size. Knead thoroughly again. Put into a buttered tin and cover and allow to rise again, until once more double the size. Bake in a hot oven for ten minutes and then reduce the heat to 350°F and bake for forty to forty-five minutes.

Cornish Pasty

½ lb. potatoes	6 oz. fat (dripping, margarine
½ lb. beefsteak	or lard)
½ teaspoonful salt	½ pint water
1 teaspoonful baking powder	1 lb. flour
1 turnip (if liked)	1 onion
1 medium-sized carrot	Pepper and salt

Peel and chop potatoes, steak, onion, carrot, and turnip. Mix salt, flour and baking powder, and rub in fat. Mix to a dough with the water, and roll out to ¼ in. thickness. Mix onion, turnip, carrot, meat and potatoes together and season with salt and pepper. Place a little of the mixture in the centre of squares of pastry and brush the edges with cold water. Fold over and press together. Bake on greased tins for about thirty to thirty-five minutes. A pleasant addition is a little chopped calves' liver.

CHAPTER TWELVE

Other Valuable Vegetables

A glance through any seedsman's catalogue or the study of some complete book on vegetables will reveal that there are a large number of unusual vegetables that can be grown in this country. It is the aim of this book, however, to concentrate on the crops that are of the greatest value from the feeding point of view and those that can be grown in any beginner's garden.

This chapter has been reserved for the vegetables that for one reason or another do not fit into the other chapters.

JERUSALEM ARTICHOKES

This is a vegetable that ought to be far more popular than it is. It is very easy to grow, and contains 7 per cent of carbohydrate.

Soil and Manuring It will grow in almost any soil, and will produce heavy crops under indifferent treatment. The heaviest yields result when the land is covered with well rotted powdery compost, added at one barrowload to 8 sq. yds. A good fish fertilizer with a 6 per cent potash content should be given at 3 oz. per sq. yd.

Planting The artichoke may be grown at the bottom of the garden, where it forms an excellent screen. It can be grown equally well alongside a fence or, of course, in rows. Because of the height of the stems, these should be 3 ft. apart. The tubers, which should be about the size of a pullet's egg, are planted 12 in. apart and 2 in. deep.

Planting is done as for potatoes.

General Cultivation When the growths are well above the soil the rows may be given some more compost or sedge peat. Towards the end of November the stems should be cut down to within a foot of the ground.

Harvesting It is possible to lift the whole crop at one time and to store the tubers in sand, but better to lift the roots as required in the winter, the egg-sized tubers being selected for planting the following season.

Varieties

New White: has a much better flavour than the old-fashioned purple.
Fuseau: the tubers are smooth and not knobbly. They are my favourite kind.

CELERY

Soil and Manuring Prepare trenches 12 in. deep and 12 in. wide and 3 ft. apart. A good layer of well rotted vegetable compost should be placed in the bottom of the trench at least 4 in. deep, and then good friable soil should be placed on top to a depth of 2 in. Liquid manure can be poured into the trench every 14 days or so with a watering can.

Seed Sowing The seed should be sown about mid-February, very thinly in boxes containing a peat-sand compost, which should be put in the greenhouse in a temperature of 60–65°F and covered with a sheet of brown paper and a sheet of glass until germination takes place. A fortnight or so later the seedlings may be pricked out into further boxes 3 in. apart. Later sowings in March can be made under continuous cloches or Access Frames, when the soil should be rich and light.

Planting   Put the seedlings out into the trenches when they are about 3–4 in. high and plant them 1 ft. apart. Firm well and then give a thorough watering.

General Cultivation   Regular waterings should be given, interspersed with feeds of liquid manure. Any side growths which appear should be removed, and the plants should be sprayed regularly with nicotine and soft soap to keep down celery fly and, if necessary, with Bordeaux mixture to prevent celery leaf spot. During the winter, protect the celery from frost with straw or bracken and bend the tops slightly to one side after the last earthing to keep the heart of the plant quite dry.

Earthing-up   Most celery has to be blanched, and the first earthing-up should be done by bringing the soil up to the base of the plant in a somewhat loose manner without allowing any soil to get between the stems. The first earthing-up is done when the plants are over 1 ft. high, the second three weeks later, and the third about six weeks later. At the last earthing-up bring the soil up to the top of the stem as high as the bottom leaves, leaving the ridges smooth and steep to enable the rain and surplus moisture to be carried away. Brown paper or corrugated cardboard can be tied round the celery plants to prevent the soil from reaching the stems.

Green celery does not require earthing up. It is grown on top of the ground and is very delicious.

Harvesting   Dig the plants up when sufficiently blanched for use in the house, and be sure to place the soil back round the dug-up portion to prevent the sticks left in the ground from greening.

Varieties

White Perfection: produces crisp, solid, firm sticks of a good flavour.

Clandon White: very thick-stemmed variety of medium height and very delicious. Is more immune to celery disease than any other type.

Clayworth Prize Pink: a large early variety which keeps well and seldom goes to seed.

Resistant Pink: a later variety which is tall and well flavoured. It is fairly resistant to celery blight.

Covent Garden Red: throws attractive red sticks which are excellent for table use.

Standard Bearer: a dark rose-coloured celery which is perhaps the tallest and largest of all varieties.

Special Note
Latterly, to save time, I have grown Greensleeves, because it doesn't require earthing-up. The stems are green when eaten. They are crisp and stringless and delicious.

CELERY, SELF-BLANCHING

Soil and Manuring The soil should be covered with compost an inch or so deep. In addition, a good fish manure or hoof and horn meal may be used at 5 oz. per sq. yd.

Seed Sowing The seed may be sown in boxes, placed on the staging of the greenhouse in a temperature of 60–65°F. A fortnight later the seedlings should be pricked out into further boxes, 3 in. apart. Those who have not got a greenhouse may sow the seed on soil over an electric hot-bed in a frame—½ oz. of seed being sufficient for a frame 6 ft. long by 4 ft. wide.

It is as well to obtain seed that has been treated with formaldehyde, as a guarantee that it is not infected with celery rust.

Those who have no facilities for seed sowing should obtain plants from a nurseryman, or should make arrangements with a reliable seedsman to supply plants at the right time.

The plants should be put out in rows 18 in. apart, and 1 ft. apart in the rows when about 4 in. tall. The ground should be well soaked afterwards. The following day the bed should be given a good hoeing, so as to leave the surface rough.

General Cultivation   Though the celery is self-bleaching, and can therefore be grown 'on the flat', it is better to place straw among the plants in the autumn so as to ensure that the stems are really white. Some people prefer to tie a stiff paper collar around each plant.

Harvesting   Dig up and use when sufficiently blanched in, say, September.

Varieties

Golden Self-Blanching: very solid—blanches easily.

LEEKS

Leeks are very valuable, for they can be used in the winter when other vegetables are scarce. Moreover, they may be dug up as required, and do not have to be lifted and stored. The severest winter cannot harm the plants.

Soil and Manuring   The leek can be grown on practically any soil. It prefers a soil in which there is plenty of organic matter and one which contains sufficient moisture.

Trenches should be got out a spade's depth, manure or other organic matter placed in the bottom, and 3 in. of good soil put on the top. This, after treading, should leave the trenches about 6 in. deep. The trenches should be 18 in. apart, and the plants put out in the trenches 1 ft. apart.

Leeks may also be grown on the flat.

In addition to the compost that is applied, dried poultry manure may be used at 2 oz. to the sq. yd., and wood ashes at 6 oz. to the sq. yd.

Top dressings of dried blood may be applied once a month throughout the season after the first two months, at 1 oz. to the sq. yd.

Seed Sowing The seed may be sown in gentle heat under glass towards the end of January. A sandy-peaty compost is bought and placed in boxes. The seed should be sown thinly on this. The boxes are then stood on the bench of the greenhouse in a temperature of about 60°F. The usual care should be taken about watering and covering the boxes with a sheet of glass and a piece of brown paper until the seedlings have germinated.

When the plants are an inch or so high they should be pricked out into other boxes filled with the Alex peat compost. The boxes should then be watered and placed on the shelf in the greenhouse, near the light, and kept at a temperature of about 55°F. When the plants are 5–6 in. high they should be gradually hardened off.

Those who have no greenhouse can sow the seed in the open about the middle of March. In the open the drills should be 8 in. apart. As soon as the seedlings can be handled they should be transplanted into another border or into a frame, 8 in. square. Here they may grow on until they are 6 in. high, when they should be planted out.

Planting The plants should be taken out of the soil carefully, so as not to break the roots. If the roots are damaged, the leaves should be cut back, so as to equalise things.

After planting in trenches 1 ft. apart, a good flooding should be given. On the flat the rows should be 1 ft. apart and the plants 8 in. apart in the rows. Holes should be made with a dibber 9 in. deep and the leeks should be dropped into the holes. A little water should be poured into the holes after planting, but the holes need not be filled in.

Another method of planting is to make drills 9 in. apart and 6 in. deep, and to plant the young leeks in these 8 in. apart.

General Cultivation   The plants grown in trenches can be earthed-up when they are half grown, say, in September.

Harvesting   Dig up as required from December onwards.

Varieties

Yates Empire: long white stems; one of the finest leeks in cultivation.

Walton Mammoth: early; mild, agreeable flavour.

Marble Pillar: dark green leaves; enormous stems; excellent flavour.

Giant Musselburgh: very popular in the Midlands; long, thick, pure white stems.

ONIONS

The onion is one of the most popular vegetables and so it is vitally important for the householder to grow sufficient for his own use. It is a vegetable that will keep quite easily. The English onion is considered more valuable than the Spanish onion and can, of course, be grown for salad purposes also.

Soil and Manuring   On the whole, onions do best on a sandy, rich loam. They will, however, do well on a heavy clay, providing this is opened up by a top dressing of finely divided organic matter.

The soil should be forked over some time before seed sowing. Composted vegetable waste should be applied at the rate of one good barrowload to 8 sq. yds. In addition, the following organic fertilizers may be added: fish manure with a 10 per cent potash content at 3 oz. to the sq. yd.; wood ashes may be used as well as $\frac{1}{2}$ lb. per sq. yd., and so may soot at $\frac{1}{4}$ lb. to the sq. yd., and dried poultry manure at 3 oz. to the sq. yd.

It is advisable to firm the surface of the soil before sowing the seed, either by treading or a light rolling. Firming should, however, never be done when the soil is sticky.

Seed Sowing—Spring During the month of March in the South, and April in the North, seed should be sown in rows 1 ft. apart and $\frac{1}{2}$ in. deep. To cover the drills it should only be necessary to give a very light raking.

General Cultivation Thinning should be done as soon as possible, so as to leave little groups 3 in. apart, and later these should be thinned to 6 in. apart. The onions thus pulled supply material for salads. Eventually these little groups are thinned down to one plant, which should produce a good bulb.

Harvesting The bulbs should ripen naturally in September, but to help them, the tops are usually bent over at the neck. After this the onions may be stored in a cool, airy, dry place. It is possible to hang them up in ropes under the shelter of the eaves of a building or in a potting or tool shed.

Seed Sowing—Autumn Seed should be sown either in the latter part of July or the beginning of August. The farther North, the earlier the sowing. For purely salad onions, the rows should be 9 in. apart, but for onions that are to bulb early, the rows should be 18 in. apart.

Such sowings usually follow the harvesting of a well manured crop, such as early peas, early potatoes, early carrots, etc., and so it is only necessary to rake the ground finely and draw out the drills.

General Cultivation   For the salad onions no thinning is done, the plants being pulled out as required. The varieties that are to bulb are thinned in the spring and the thinnings transplanted, 12 in. between the rows and 6–9 in. between the plants.

Harvesting   They should be ready for use in August.

Seed Sowing—Pickling   Those who have an odd corner of poor soil and wish to grow onions with little or no soil preparation should grow pickling onions.

The seed should be broadcast over the surface of the soil in April and lightly raked in. The crop is kept weeded, but is not thinned.

Harvesting   Pickling onions are ready in September as a rule.

Varieties

Spring Sown
Bedfordshire Champion: produces a good-sized bulb of mild flavour.
Wizbo: an excellent keeper; golden brown skin; ball shaped; a very heavy cropper.
Ailsa Craig: a good all-round variety.

Autumn-Sown Salad
White Lisbon: the favourite silver-skinned variety for pulling green.
The Queen: should be grown where White Lisbon is subject to disease.

Autumn-Sown Bulbing
Unwins Reliance: a long keeping onion of good size. Ripens in the summer.

Pickling
The Queen: small and very quick growing.

SHALLOTS

As shallots are one of the easiest vegetables to grow, and are not as a rule attacked by the onion fly, they will prove an excellent crop for the beginner.

Soil and Manuring   Shallots will grow on almost any soil, providing it has been well worked and is well drained. Organic manures may be applied as advised for onions, and, in addition, hoof and horn meal or a good fish manure may be forked into the top few inches at the rate of 5–6 oz. to the sq. yd.

Planting   In the South it should be possible to get the planting done early in February, and in the North during the second or third week of March. The rows should be 1 ft. apart and the bulbs spaced out 4 in. apart in the rows.

Before planting, the soil should be firmed, and the bulbs then pushed in to half their depth. Any loose skins or dead tops should be removed. A fortnight after planting, the bed should be examined and the bulbs firmed again if necessary. Any that have gone rotten should be replaced.

Planting can be done in any odd place—for instance, along the tops of celery trenches, as an edging to a path, or in between rows of fruit bushes.

General Cultivation   The rows should be hoed if necessary, but not deeply. Care should be taken not to bury the bulbs.

Harvesting   In July the leaves of the shallot will be seen to be turning yellow, and by the second or third week the bulbs should be lifted and left on the surface of the soil to dry off. After a few days they may be placed on a path or a concrete yard in the sun. They should be turned over two or three times so as to make certain they are thoroughly dry. After this the clusters of bulbs should be separated into single bulbs and stored in a cool, dry place.

Varieties

Dutch yellow: produces a larger and rounder bulb than the true variety. The skin is coppery red and the leaves are greyish-green. Yields a heavy crop, but does not keep as well as the true shallot.

True Red Shallot: produces a nice firm bulb of the right size for pickling. Keeps well.

SPINACH

A very valuable vegetable, for it is rich in vitamins A, B1, and B2. It is moderately high in calorific value, and contains a percentage of iron, calcium and phosphorus.

There are various kinds: Summer, Winter, Spinach Beet, Seakale and New Zealand Spinach; and these will all be dealt with under separate headings.

ANNUAL SPINACH—SUMMER AND WINTER

Soil and Manuring　The annual spinach will grow almost anywhere. It goes to seed quickly on very light soils, and to prevent this plenty of compost, which of course is moisture-holding material, should be incorporated.

When preparing the ground, powdery composted vegetable refuse may be applied at the rate of one good barrow-load to 8 sq. yds. In addition, meat and bone, hoof and horn, or a good fish manure may be raked into the ground at the rate of 4 oz. to the sq. yd. Dried blood may be given in very small dressings along the rows three times at fortnightly intervals, directly the plants have been growing for several weeks.

Seed Sowing　Summer Spinach should be sown once a fortnight from the beginning of March onwards, in order to keep up the supply. As the weather gets warmer the sowings should be made in the shadier situations of the garden. In a small garden quite short rows will do. The drills should be 18 in. apart and 1 in. deep, and directly the seedlings can be handled they should be thinned out to 6 in. apart.

Winter Spinach should be sown from the first week in August to the middle of September, once a fortnight. It is often necessary in the North and West to make special raised beds of 5 ft. wide, 3 in. above the level of the soil around. This keeps the beds dry. Under this system the rows should be 9 in. apart and the seedlings are thinned to 4 in. apart.

General Cultivation The Winter Spinach may need protection. This can be done by using straw over and between the rows. Bracken or heather is useful too, and so, of course, are continuous cloches.

Harvesting Summer Spinach should be picked regularly and quite hard. It does not matter if the majority of leaves are removed from a plant.

Winter Spinach should not be picked hard. The largest leaves should be taken, and these should be gathered singly.

Varieties

Summer
Monarch Long Standing: a round-seeded variety. Does not easily go to seed.
The Round Victoria: perhaps the broadest-leaved, round-seeded spinach grown.

Winter
Long Standing New Prickly: for winter and spring use. Is hardy and crops heavily.

SPINACH BEET

This is a perpetual spinach and produces a continuous supply of large leaves during spring, summer and autumn.

Soil and Manuring   (See Beetroot, p. 56).

Seed Sowing   The seed should be sown in April, and another sowing in August. In this way it should be possible to pick spinach all the year. The rows should be 18 in. apart and the plants should be thinned out to 18 in. apart in the rows.

General Cultivation   Regular weeding, if necessary, and occasional waterings are all that are necessary to keep the plants cropping satisfactorily.

Harvesting   The leaves should be gathered regularly directly they are large enough. If this is not done the older leaves will begin to get coarse. It is necessary to pick the leaves, stem and all, so as to ensure further leaves developing.

SEAKALE SPINACH

The Seakale Beet or Seakale Spinach is grown for the thick white stems it produces and for the large green leaves growing at the ends of these stems. The latter are used as spinach, and the former as seakale.

Soil and Manuring   (See Beetroot, p. 56).

Seed Sowing   Seeds should be sown thinly late in April or early in May, in drills 15 in. apart. Plants should be spaced out to 9 in. apart in the rows.

General Cultivation   As for Spinach Beet—see above.

Harvesting   The leaves and stems should be pulled regularly and should not be cut. If the leaves are removed without the stems, cropping is impeded.

VEGETABLE MARROW

The marrow is a crop that is quite easy to grow in any odd corner. It is quite suitable for covering up a mound or for growing up a fence, or even up wire-netting. In the latter case it has to be tied into position, for its tendrils are not really sufficient to support the stems when carrying those heavy fruits.

Soil and Manuring   If the crop can follow one which has been liberally manured, there is no special cultivation to be done. As much organic matter as possible should, however, be used, and, in addition, bone meal should be applied at 2 oz. per sq. yd., and wood ashes at 4 oz. per sq. yd.

Seed Sowing   It is usual to sow seeds in 3 in. pots in a greenhouse, early in April, and the plants are thus quite ready to be put out into open ground towards the end of May.

Those who have no greenhouse may sow seed in frames or in a little pocket of specially prepared soil outside where the plants are to grow. The little pockets should be prepared with plenty of organic matter, and a glass jam jar should be placed over them in order to help germination and to give the seedlings some protection when they come through. It is inadvisable to sow the seed much before the first week of May.

Planting   Where numbers of marrows are to be grown, the plants should be placed 3 ft. apart in the rows, and if there are to be numbers of rows, the rows should be 6 ft. apart. Bush marrows are preferable under this system. Trailers grown under such conditions have to be kept pinched back. It is on the rubbish heap and the odd corner that they may be allowed to ramble as they like.

6   Marrow seeds are sown where they are to grow. They are covered
    with jam jars until the plants touch the tops. They can be allowed
    to roam along the ground or encouraged to climb.

General Cultivation   Hoeing should be done regularly
and top dressings of sedge peat given during June.

Harvesting   Marrows should be cut when they are young
and tender, for then the plants will produce a heavier crop.
Regular cutting may treble a crop.

Varieties

Long White: a white, trailing type, bearing a large, smooth marrow with no rib or neck.

Bush-shaped Green: bears medium-sized fruits.

Bush-shaped White: similar to above, but creamy-white.

Custard: bears flattened fruits with scalloped edges, and of a delicious flavour.

CHAPTER THIRTEEN

Other Valuable Vegetable Recipes

This is the chapter in which many valuable vegetables appear. The Jerusalem artichoke is the first, and unfortunately this is a crop which is not known or grown enough in this country. The carbohydrate it contains is most digestible, and it is also of great value in providing vitamin B.

Celery has always been noted for its health-giving constituents. It contains vitamin C and has the great advantage, of course, that it can be eaten raw as well as cooked. It is the vegetable that is always said to be of great value in the control of rheumatism. The advantage of growing one's own celery is that if it is freshly dug, quickly washed, and served almost immediately, it is much more flavoursome and richer in food value than if it is bought in a shop several days after it has been dug up.

The leek is one of the few vegetables that has never suffered from unpopularity in this country. Right from the earliest days it has been a crop that has appeared on the table of both rich and poor. It is particularly popular in the North, and the only 'snag' seems to be the soil grittiness that is difficult to wash out when preparing this vegetable. When blanching is carried out with brown paper, the soil never actually touches the roots. Even the outer leaves of the leek can be used as a flavouring for soups, stews, etc.

Onions have great food value. If found to be indigestible,

they should be sliced and eaten raw. They are then quite digestible.

Spinach is another very important crop which should be more widely grown. It is valuable for its alkaline salts, and contains vitamins A, B2 and C. If it disagrees with some people when cooked, it is excellent when eaten raw in a salad.

The vegetable marrow, the last of the vegetables mentioned in this chapter, though containing a quantity of water, is also full of invaluable salts, and is as useful, in fact, as runner beans or cauliflower. Marrows can be eaten when they are young or when they are fully ripened and have been stored for some time. They are, in fact, both a summer and winter vegetable.

JERUSALEM ARTICHOKES

Boiled Artichokes

> 2 lb. artichokes   ½ pint water
> ½ pint white sauce   Salt
> ½ pint milk

Wash the artichokes, peel them, and place them in water to which a little vinegar has been added. Have ready sufficient boiling milk and water (equal quantities) just to cover the artichokes. Put in a pinch of salt. Boil gently with the lid on for fifteen to twenty minutes. Strain and place in a hot dish. Serve with melted butter sauce or white sauce. The liquor left can be utilized for soup.

Fried Artichokes

Wash the artichokes thoroughly in cold water, peel them, and put them into cold water to which a little vinegar has been added. Slice them thickly, and then place in a large saucepan of boiling water. Boil for fifteen minutes. Drain well, dip each slice in frying batter, and fry until a deep golden colour. Serve very hot.

Baked Artichokes

> *1 lb. artichokes*   *Pepper and salt*
> *1 oz. margarine or butter*

Peel and trim the artichokes neatly and dry them well. Melt the fat in a baking dish and place the artichokes in this, seasoning with the pepper and salt. Bake in a moderate oven for about half an hour, basting frequently.

Artichoke Soup

> *1 pint white stock*   *½ pint milk*
> *1½ lb. artichokes*   *1 oz. margarine or butter*
> *1 onion*   *Pepper and salt*

Peel onion and artichokes and place in cold water with a few drops of lemon juice. Slice finely into a pan with the melted margarine or butter. Toss lightly until they have absorbed this, and then add the stock. Simmer for half an hour. Rub through a sieve. Serve with toast.

Artichoke Pie

Mash the cooked artichokes, or rub them through a sieve, adding a little lemon juice and some onion purée. Put alternate layers of this mixture and grated cheese in a pie dish. Cover the top with breadcrumbs and cheese and a few dabs of margarine or butter. Bake in a hot oven for ten minutes.

Artichoke Soufflé

Cook the artichokes and rub through a sieve. Make a sauce with the liquor, and then take equal quantities of the purée and sauce, and the yolks of two eggs, mix well together and beat quickly. Just before putting the mixture into the oven, fold in the whites of the two eggs beaten to a stiff froth. Sprinkle the top with finely grated Parmesan cheese and bake for twenty minutes.

Cheese Artichokes

Cook the artichokes and cut them into slices. Put into a dish and cover with a thick white sauce, made from the liquor in which they have been boiled and to which some grated cheese and the yolk of an egg have been added. Season with pepper, and brown quickly in the oven.

Artichoke Mould

1 lb. artichokes	*Tomato or cheese sauce*
2 eggs	*1 oz. margarine or butter*
½ pint milk	*Pepper and salt*

Boil the artichokes in the milk, mash them well, and pass through a fine sieve. Add the margarine or butter, the eggs (well beaten), salt and pepper, pour into a well greased mould, and steam for one hour. Serve with white sauce, or tomato sauce, poured over.

CELERY

Braised Celery

3 heads of celery	*1 carrot*
2 oz. bacon	*1 pint stock*
1 small onion	*Pepper and salt*

Wash and trim the heads of celery and blanch in boiling salted water for five minutes. Drain and place in a saucepan over the sliced bacon, sliced onion and sliced carrot. Pour over the pint of stock. Season with salt and pepper, cover and simmer for 1½ hours.

Creamed Celery

1 good head of celery	*1 oz. margarine or butter*
1 pint milk	*1 oz. flour*
1 teaspoonful salt	*4 oz. grated cheese*
Breadcrumbs	*Pepper*

Wash the celery and cut enough into small dice to fill a pint measure. Cook with the milk and salt until tender. Drain off. In another pan melt the margarine or butter and mix in the flour. Add the milk gradually, keeping well stirred. Boil for three or four minutes, then add the grated cheese, pepper and celery. Bring to boil again and serve with breadcrumbs fried in a little fat until they are golden brown. Serve very hot.

Fried Celery

> *1 head of celery*   *Batter*
> *Fat for frying*

Prepare the celery. Cut into short lengths and boil in salted water until tender. Have the batter ready and dip each piece in this, frying until lightly browned. This should take about four minutes.

Celery Soup (i)

> *1 head of celery*   *¾ pint boiling water*
> *1 onion*   *1 pint milk*
> *1½ oz. margarine or butter* *Toast*
> *1 oz. flour*   *Pepper and salt*

Wash and cut up the celery. Boil with the onion until tender. Rub through a sieve, and melt the margarine or butter and mix into the flour, adding the cold milk and the celery purée, and boil for eight minutes. Serve with toast.

Celery Soup (ii)

> *1 good head of celery*   *½ pint milk*
> *1 pint stock*   *1 egg*
> *1 onion*   *1 teaspoonful lemon juice*

Wash and prepare celery. Boil with the onion in salted water and lemon juice. Drain well and rub through a fine sieve. Return to saucepan and add stock. Boil up quickly. Just before serving, add the egg (well beaten) and the milk.

Celery-Leaf Salad

Wash and dry fresh young celery leaves. Sprinkle lightly with salad oil. Garnish with slices of tomato and beetroot. Pour over French dressing or mayonnaise.

Tomato and Celery Salad

Peel the tomatoes and cut the flesh into thin strips. Mix these with strips of celery, sprinkle with finely chopped onion, and serve with salad dressing and mustard.

Celery Pie

Wash and cook the celery. With the liquid in which it was boiled, make a thick white sauce by adding 1 oz. of flour, ½ oz. margarine or butter, the yolk of an egg and a little milk. Do not let the mixture actually boil after adding the egg, or it will curdle. Put a layer of celery into a pie dish, then a layer of sauce, followed by a layer of finely grated cheese. Sprinkle breadcrumbs over the top and bake in a hot oven until browned.

Scrambled Eggs and Celery

1 head of celery	*2 oz. margarine or butter*
3 eggs	*Pepper and salt*

Wash and cook the celery. Rub through a sieve. Beat the eggs thoroughly and add the sieved celery. Put into a pan containing the boiling fat and stir until it reaches the required consistency. Serve on hot buttered toast.

Scalloped Celery

Wash and cook the celery. Cut into pieces about 2 in. long. Put into a greased dish and cover with a sauce made as follows: 1 oz. margarine or butter mixed with 1 oz. flour and three-quarters of the liquid in which the celery has been boiled. Cover with browned breadcrumbs. Bake in a quick oven.

Stuffed Celery

2 heads of celery	2 oz. margarine or butter
3 oz. grated cheese	Pepper and salt

Mix the cheese thoroughly with the butter or margarine. Wash the celery thoroughly and split open the heads. Fill the hollow parts with the cheese mixture. Press the heads well together again and serve cut into broad rings.

Celery and Macaroni

2 heads of celery	1 oz. macaroni
1 bay leaf	Pepper and salt
½ pint white sauce	

Wash and trim the celery. Boil until tender in milk and water seasoned with salt and pepper and a bay leaf. Drain and cut into 2 in. lengths. Cook the macaroni and cut into similar lengths. Heat the sauce and mix the celery and macaroni into this. Simmer gently for about a quarter of an hour, and serve very hot.

Celery and Cheese

Braise the celery by allowing 4 oz. of butter to 3 lb. of celery and covering with half a tumbler of water. Season and simmer in a covered dish for about two hours or until tender. Make a cheese sauce by melting some chopped cheese in a little milk with a knob of butter. Add pepper and salt, a 'drop' of vinegar, and a pinch of mustard. Pour this over the celery and, after sprinkling grated cheese on top, brown under the grill.

LEEKS

Buttered Leeks

Trim the leeks and cook in boiling salted water until tender. A little vinegar added to the water helps to keep them a good colour. When cooked, drain and fry in boiling fat until lightly browned.

Braised Leeks

Prepare the leeks and put them in a casserole. Sprinkle with salt and pepper, add 2 oz. of margarine or butter and a little water. The juice of a small lemon also improves the flavour. Simmer gently for 1–1½ hours, keeping the lid closed.

Leeks and Toast

Trim the leeks and wash them thoroughly. Boil until tender, and when cooked halve them and arrange on a very hot dish. Pour over a thick white sauce or a good brown gravy. Served with buttered toast these are delicious.

Leek and Potato Soup

3 leeks	2 oz. margarine or butter
½ lb. potatoes	1¼ pints milk
1 egg	Some fried bread

Peel the potatoes and cut into quarters. Cut the leeks into slices and fry until soft—not browned. Add the potatoes and about 1 pint of hot milk. Season with salt and boil for about twenty minutes. Put the mixture through a sieve, return to the pan, and simmer gently for another ten minutes. Then take the saucepan off the stove and add the egg, well beaten with the milk, and also the margarine or butter. Serve with fried bread cut up into small squares.

Leeks and Cheese

Wash the leeks and cut into even lengths. Cook until tender and arrange in a greased pie dish. Pour on a thick white sauce and cover with grated cheese. Finish off the top with small dabs of margarine or butter. Brown in the oven and serve very hot.

Cockie Leekie

An old hen
4 large leeks
2 tablespoonsful vinegar
1 tablespoonful chopped parsley
¼ lb. prunes
½ cupful rice
Pepper and salt

Clean the hen, put in water and a little vinegar, and allow to stand. After washing again, simmer until tender. Add the rice, leeks, salt and pepper, and simmer until thoroughly cooked. Then add the prunes, without the syrup. (These should be stewed and stoned.) Add the chopped parsley. Take out the hen, leaving a few pieces of the breast in the soup. Serve very hot. The meat should be removed from the bones, and if sent to the table covered with white sauce, it can be served as a separate dish.

Egg-and-Milk Leeks

4 leeks
2 oz. margarine or butter
3 rashers of bacon
1 egg
1 pint milk or milk and water
1 oz. flour
Pepper and salt

Stew the leeks slowly in the milk, or milk and water. Make a sauce with the margarine or butter, flour and milk. Remove from the stove, add the egg, and stir for a few seconds. Put the leeks on to a very hot dish and pour the sauce over. Decorate with the rashers of bacon, crisply fried.

Poached Eggs and Leeks

4 leeks
½ carrot
1 bay leaf
½ oz. flour
½ pint of milk
1 onion
½ turnip
2 oz. margarine or butter
½ pint of stock
3 poached eggs
Pepper and salt

Cut the onion, carrot and turnip into thin slices. Cook the leeks until tender. Heat half the margarine or butter in a pan and add the leeks, onion, carrot, bay leaf and turnip, and fry slowly for ten minutes. Add the stock, cover and cook for one hour. Make a white sauce with the milk, remainder of the margarine or butter, flour, and any stock that may be left. Take out the leeks and cut them lengthwise into four. Place them on hot buttered toast, pouring the sauce over and arranging the poached eggs around it.

ONIONS

Boiled Onions

4 onions	*White sauce*
Parsley	*Pepper and salt*
	Prepared gravy

Peel and wash the onions. Place in a pan of cold water and bring to the boil. Drain off and rinse in cold water. Put the gravy into the saucepan, replace the onions and boil gently for 1½ hours. Season with salt and pepper and thicken with flour. Put the onions on a hot dish, pour the sauce round, and serve very hot.

Nantwich 'Acton' Onions

Select medium, even-sized onions. Peel and wash them. Place in a saucepan of deep brown beef fat and bring to the boil and simmer until tender. Drain and serve on a hot dish. The onions do not taste greasy, as may be imagined, but they do absorb the subtle flavour of the dripping.

Roasted Onions

Trim the tops and roots from the onions and peel them. Boil them gently in salted water until nearly done. Drain and dry them and put in a tin with a little dripping. Roast for about twenty minutes, turning occasionally.

Fried Onions

Peel and slice the onions finely. Season with salt and pepper. Have ready a pan of very hot oil or fat. Toss the onions into this. Stir continually whilst frying, and fry until they are a golden brown.

Stewed Onions

4 onions	Pepper and salt
1 pint stock or brown gravy	

Peel and trim the onions, place in cold water, bring to the boil, and strain. Place in a pan again with the stock, and then simmer gently for about 1½ hours.

Onion Soup (i)

2 onions	1 pint milk
1 oz. margarine or butter	Pepper and salt

Boil the onions in milk until tender. Mash them up in the liquor, adding the salt and pepper and the margarine or butter. Serve very hot.

Onion Soup (ii)

6 onions	2 oz. cheese
1 egg	Pepper and salt
2 oz. margarine or butter	

Slice the onions and fry until golden brown. Add 1½ pints of hot water and boil until the liquid has been reduced by one-third. Beat the egg and add gradually, after removing pan from heat. Add the margarine or butter, season with salt and pepper. Serve with grated cheese.

Onion Soup (iii)

½ lb. onions	1 pint stock
2 oz. margarine or butter	½ teaspoonful castor sugar
Fried bread	Pepper and salt

Peel and fry the onions, not browning them. Add the sugar, stock and the salt and pepper. Boil for twenty minutes. Serve with fried bread cut up fine.

Onion Soup (iv)

2 large onions	*2 oz. flour*
1 large potato	*½ pint milk*
3 pieces celery	*1 pint water*
2 oz. butter	*Pepper and salt*

Peel and slice the onions, potato and celery. Melt the butter and fry the vegetables gently for ten minutes, not browning them. Add milk and water and simmer for one hour, then rub through a sieve, and return to saucepan. Mix the flour with a little milk until smooth, pour into the soup and simmer for ten minutes. Season to taste and serve with fingers of toast.

Onion Salad

Spring onions are often served separately as a salad, but they can be added, thinly sliced, or whole if they are small, to almost any kind of salad to give it a distinctive flavour. It should be remembered, though, that not everyone likes onions, and therefore if visitors are expected, the most satisfactory way is to serve onions separately in a bowl so that those who like them may help themselves.

Golden Rings

4 large onions	*Oil for frying*
2 tablespoonsful flour	*Salt and pepper to taste*

Peel the onions and cut into rings ¼ in. thick; see that these rings are separate and *are* rings! Put the oil in a pan; make this smoking hot. Coat the rings with a little flour seasoned with pepper and salt, drop them into the deep fat and fry a golden brown. Lift out and drain.

Onion Fritters

4 oz. flour	Water to mix
3 onions	1 medium-sized marrow
½ teaspoonful curry powder	Salt

Make a batter of the flour and water and beat thoroughly. Peel the marrow and cut it into strips about 3 in. long. Peel and slice the onions and mix with the marrow. Add this mixture to the batter. Have ready a deep pan of heated fat. Drop a pinch of mustard into the batter and stir well, and then drop spoonsful into the hot fat and fry until a golden brown.

Stuffed Onions (i)

4 large onions	¼ lb. cooked meat
¼ pint brown sauce	2 tablespoonsful breadcrumbs
½ teaspoonful yeast extract	Pepper and salt
Margarine or butter	

Peel and partly cook the onions in salted water. Scoop out their centres and chop them up finely. Mince the cooked meat and add the breadcrumbs. Mix the chopped onion into this. Melt the yeast extract in the brown sauce or gravy and mix with the onion mixture. Fill the centres of the onions and pile up on the top. Place a small dab of margarine or butter on the top of each, and bake slowly in the oven until tender.

Stuffed Onions (ii)

4 onions	½ lb. sausage meat
3 oz. margarine or butter	Pepper and salt

Peel the onions and put them in a saucepan of cold water—just enough to cover them. Bring this to the boil, and then strain off the water. Rinse the onions in cold water, and then put them into a saucepan of boiling salted water and boil until they are tender. Take them out and drain well. Then scoop out the centres, filling them with sausage meat. Put the margarine or butter into a baking tin and melt it. Place the onions in this and bake until nicely browned. Serve garnished with parsley.

Stuffed Onions (iii)

2 lb. onions	1 oz. breadcrumbs
1 egg yolk	1 pinch celery salt
2 oz. chopped walnuts	1 teaspoonful salt

Peel and boil the onions until tender, but do not allow them to split. Drain and rinse with plenty of cold water. Remove the centres. Chop them and add to the other ingredients mentioned above. Mix together and season to taste. Pile into the onions. Arrange in a greased dish and then bake for half an hour.

Stuffed Onions (iv)

8 large onions	½ teaspoonful dried sage
12 oz. pig's liver	Pinch black pepper
3 oz. butter	Salt to taste

Peel the onions and trim off just enough of the bottoms to enable them to stand upright. Remove the centres and tie a band of greaseproof paper round each onion. Place in baking dish. Chop the liver coarsely with some of the scooped-out onion, the sage, pepper and salt. Place a small knob of butter into each onion and almost fill with the liver mixture. Melt remaining butter and pour over each onion. Cover with foil and bake slowly for 1½ hours or until tender. Remove foil, increase heat and cook until the tops are nicely browned. Remove greaseproof paper carefully before serving.

Onion Toast

3 onions	Mustard
Toast	Pepper and salt
3 oz. cheese	

Peel the onions and slice finely. Fry in boiling fat until nicely browned. Season with the salt and pepper, and put thickly on to slices of buttered toast. Slice the cheese thinly and place a layer over each slice of toast. Put a little mustard on each piece and heat until the cheese is melted. Serve very hot.

Baked Onions and Brown Sauce

> 3 large onions
> Chopped parsley
> ½ pint brown sauce
>
> ½ oz. margarine or butter
> Pepper and salt

Take from the onions the roots and tops and any rough skin. Place them in a baking tin with a little margarine or butter and bake until practically cooked. Peel them and cut in halves. Put them into a casserole, pour over the sauce, and cook gently for fifteen minutes. Serve on a heated dish garnished with chopped parsley.

Onion Porridge

> ½ lb. onions
> 1 tablespoonful butter
>
> 1 pint water
> Pepper and salt

Prepare the onions by careful peeling, dividing them into four pieces after such preparation. Put in a saucepan with the butter, salt to taste, and two breakfastcupsful of cold water. Boil gently until onions are tender, then stir in a pinch of salt and a sprinkling of pepper. Pour into a warmed basin and serve very hot at bedtime to cure a cold.

Onion and Cheese Savoury

> 4 large onions
> ¼ lb. of cheese
>
> 1 small knob of butter
> Pepper, salt and mustard

Peel the onions and cut in ½ in. thick slices. Grease a baking dish with the butter, lay the onion slices in flat, dust them with pepper and salt; place dish in moderately hot oven, bake until tender (say 35 minutes). When cooked through, cover each slice with cheese, grated and seasoned with pepper. Put again in oven to cook and lightly brown the cheese. Serve with freshly-made mustard, or you can transfer the onions and cheese to mounds of buttered toast, or on to small rounds of mashed potatoes.

Onion and Potato Hot-Pot

1 lb. onions   *2 oz. margarine or butter*
1 pint hot water   *Yeast extract*
1 lb. potatoes   *Pepper and salt*

Peel and slice the onions. Place in a pan of boiling water and boil gently for ten minutes, then drain off. Grease a dish and put half the margarine or butter into this. Peel the potatoes and slice them thinly. Place layers of onion and layers of potatoes on top. Mix the yeast extract in the hot water and pour over the onion-and-potato mixture. Add the remainder of the margarine or butter, place a lid on the pan, and cook in a moderate oven for about an hour. About ten minutes before serving, the lid may be removed so that the potatoes on top may be browned.

Onion Flan

1½ lb. onions   *Short pastry*
3 oz. cheese   *½ teaspoonful black pepper*
2 eggs   *Salt to taste*
1 tablespoonful butter

Peel and slice the onions thinly. Toss in heated butter in frying pan and fry gently for fifteen minutes until golden brown and almost cooked. Remove from heat and when slightly cooled mix in the beaten eggs, grated cheese, pepper and salt. Line a flan tin with the pastry and fill with onion mixture. Cook for twenty minutes and serve immediately.

Onion Crisps

2 medium-sized onions per person   *Pepper and salt*
Oil for frying

Peel and slice the onions into thick rings. Roll the onion in flour seasoned with pepper and salt. Heat the oil, and deep

7 Cooking onion crisps.

fry the onions until they are crisp. Drain well and serve with fingers of buttered toast.

Tripe and Onions

1½ lb. dressed tripe	¾ pint milk
4 large onions	1 teacupful water
1½ oz. flour	Pepper and salt

Cut the tripe into 3 or 4 in. squares. Cover with cold water and bring to boil. Strain, and return the tripe to the saucepan. Slice the onions thinly and add them to the tripe with the milk, cold water and salt. Simmer for three hours. Half an hour before serving, mix the flour with a little milk, salt and pepper and stir into the tripe and onions. Simmer for twenty minutes and serve immediately.

Tioro

1½ lb. onions	2 cloves garlic
1 lb. gurnet	3 tablespoonsful olive oil
¾ lb. cod	Pinch black pepper
1 tablespoonful finely chopped parsley	Salt

Wash the fish and cut into neat pieces. Dust with pepper and salt and brown lightly in a little olive oil; place in the bottom of a heatproof dish. Fry the peeled and sliced garlic cloves until dark brown and shrunken, then remove them. In the flavoured oil, fry the peeled and sliced onion until golden brown, stir in a little black pepper and pile on top of the fish. Cover with foil and cook in moderate oven until the fish is cooked. Meanwhile make enough toast to cover a serving dish and arrange the fish and onions, together with all juices, on the toast and serve at once.

Boiled Onions Au Gratin

2 medium-sized onions per person	*White sauce*
Grated cheese	*Breadcrumbs*

Peel the onions, place in cold water, bring to boil and strain. Place onions in another saucepan of boiling salted water and boil until tender then strain. Put in a hot dish and cover with white sauce. Sprinkle with the cheese and breadcrumbs and place under a hot grill until golden brown. Serve immediately.

Dried Onion Rings

Choose large onions. Remove the outer skins. Place the onions on a board and, starting at the bottom end, cut crosswise in slices, taking care to keep these slices of uniform thickness, i.e. five or six to the inch. Lay the slices on trays of butter-muslin and dry in a hot oven, keeping the door ajar an inch or two. A muslin drying tray is easily made. Have a framework of thin wooden lathes, made to fit your oven. The muslin is cut out in two layers and stretched and tacked firmly to the sides and ends of this frame.

A lot of onion rings can be evaporated for storing and, once dried, they may be packed in brown paper bags and hung up somewhere dry. As they have had the moisture evaporated from them and have not been baked in any way, these onion rings are like fresh onions within half an hour of being placed in cold water. They are then ready to cook for stews, curries or other dishes.

SHALLOTS

Shallots are generally used as a pickle, but there is no reason at all why they should not be utilized in any dish where onions are normally used. Used thus they are both useful and appetizing.

SPINACH

Boiled Spinach (i)

> 2 lb. spinach   Pepper and salt
> 1 oz. margarine or butter

Strip the leaves from the stalks of the spinach and wash very carefully in several waters. Take the spinach from the water and put it into an empty saucepan. Cover closely and cook very slowly for about thirty minutes. Stir frequently. When cooked, take it out of the pan and squeeze as much moisture from it as possible. Rub through a sieve and add the margarine or butter and the pepper and salt. Put back into the saucepan and reheat. Serve with croûtons of fried bread.

Boiled Spinach (ii)

> 2 lb. spinach   1 oz. margarine or butter
> Fried bread   Pepper and salt
> 2 oz. flour

Prepare the spinach, thoroughly washing it to free from grit. Put into a saucepan with sufficient water just to cover the bottom of the pan, adding half a tablespoonful of salt. Boil for twenty minutes, keeping the lid off. When cooked rub it through a sieve, mix in the margarine or butter, pepper, salt, and sprinkle in the flour. Place in a pan and cook over a gentle heat for about six minutes, stirring continually. Serve very hot, with toast or fried bread.

Spinach Soup

> 1½ lb. spinach   1 oz. margarine or butter
> 1 pint stock   1 oz. flour
> ½ pint milk   Pepper and salt

Wash the spinach thoroughly and cook with just enough water to cover the bottom of the saucepan. When tender, drain off and rub through a sieve, adding the margarine and sprinkling in the flour. Mix with the stock, and boil for a few minutes. Add the milk, stirring continually, and boil very gently for a further five minutes. Season with salt and pepper and serve with snippets of toast.

Egg and Spinach Salad

2 hard-boiled eggs	Vinegar
½ lb. young spinach	1 tablespoonful salad oil
4 spring onions	Pepper and salt

Wash the spinach thoroughly. Dry it and mix with the onions, which should be finely chopped. Put a few drops of vinegar into the salad oil, season with salt and pepper, and mix well together. Pour this over the spinach and put the whole into a salad bowl. Cut the eggs into slices and garnish the spinach.

Spinach Fritters

1 lb. spinach	2 eggs
¼ pint white sauce	Nutmeg
2 oz. margarine or butter	Pepper and salt

Wash and cook the spinach in just a little water, and when tender, drain well and chop finely, or put through a sieve. Reheat and add the white sauce, the eggs (well beaten), and salt and pepper to season. A slight trace of grated nutmeg improves the flavour. Have ready a pan of boiling fat and drop spoonfuls of the spinach mixture into it, cooking until they are a golden brown. They should be served very hot.

Poached Eggs and Spinach

2 lb. spinach	Toast
3 poached eggs	Pepper and salt

Prepare and cook the spinach as in the preceding recipe. Poach the eggs and trim them to a good round shape. Place each on a slice of toast and surround with the spinach purée.

Spinach Toast

2 lb. spinach	1 oz. margarine or butter
2 oz. flour	Fried bread or toast
½ pint brown gravy	Pepper and salt

Prepare and cook the spinach in a little water. Rub through a sieve or chop finely and place in a pan with the margarine or butter, the gravy and the salt and pepper. Sprinkle in the flour and stir gently over the fire until the mixture thickens to a creamy consistency. Pile this on the slices of fried bread or toast and serve hot.

Spinach and Lettuce Soup

6 spinach leaves	4 dozen fried croûtons of toast
1 lettuce	1 teaspoonful freshly ground pepper
Green part from 2 leeks	1 level teaspoonful salt
1 lb. shelled peas	A pinch of sugar
A few sprigs of chervil	¼ pint water
3 oz. butter	2 pints vegetable stock

Wash the spinach, lettuce and leeks. Shred them all afterwards. Put them with the peas, chervil, pepper, salt, sugar, butter and a little water, in the saucepan. Bring to the boil. Cover. Simmer for about forty minutes, adding a little more water if necessary. Sieve well. Return to the pan and bring to the boil. Add the boiling stock. Serve with the fried croûtons.

Spinach Dumplings

2 rashers bacon	1 small onion
2 tablespoonsful butter	1 egg
8 oz. white bread	4 tablespoonsful flour
¼ pint milk	Left-over spinach
¼ pint water	Salt

Cut the bread into dice; fry them in the butter and then soak in ½ pint of milk and water, and beat with one egg. Add four tablespoonsful of flour, a little salt, the left-over spinach, and one small onion which must be chopped up and fried brown in a little butter. Form with floured hands, dumplings of round balls of spinach the size of, say, a walnut. Boil the dumplings in salted water for about fifteen minutes. Cut up the bacon rashers in small dice; fry them and then pour them, with the fat, over the dumplings.

SPINACH BEET

This is treated in the same way as ordinary spinach, and any of the foregoing recipes for spinach also apply to spinach beet.

SEAKALE SPINACH

The recipes for spinach can also be used for seakale spinach. It must be remembered, however, that with the seakale spinach there is a broad, white, thick mid-rib which acts as the stalk of the spinach-like leaf. This thick ivory stalk can be cooked as seakale, and should be served with a white sauce, the leaf being cooked as spinach. Thus you have two vegetables in one.

VEGETABLE MARROW

Boiled Marrow

1 vegetable marrow	*White sauce*
½ pint milk	*Pepper and salt*
2 oz. margarine or butter	

Peel the marrow and remove the seeds; cut up and rinse in cold water. Melt the margarine or butter in a pan, put in the marrow, and season with pepper and salt. Cook gently over a low heat with the lid on for about half an hour. Make the white sauce from milk and the liquid in which the marrow has simmered.

For this method the marrows must be very young and tender. Older marrows should be boiled in plenty of water.

Fried Marrow

> *1 marrow*   *2 oz. margarine or butter*
> *Breadcrumbs*   *1 egg*

Peel the marrow, remove the seeds, and cut into slices. Beat the egg and mix with the breadcrumbs. Coat each piece of marrow, and fry in the margarine or butter until lightly browned. Serve hot on a heated dish.

Mashed Marrow

> *1 medium-sized marrow*   *1 oz. flour*
> *1 tablespoonful milk*   *Pepper and salt*
> *1 oz. margarine or butter*

Peel the marrow and remove the seeds. Boil until tender in salted water and mash well, or rub through a sieve. Melt the margarine or butter in a saucepan, add the marrow, milk, salt and pepper. Sprinkle in the flour gradually, stirring all the time until the mixture thickens to a creamy consistency.

Marrow Soup

> *1 marrow*   *½ pint milk*
> *1 egg*   *Pepper and salt*

Peel and remove the seeds from the marrow. Boil in salted water until tender, and when cooked rub through a sieve. Beat the egg and add to the marrow, mixing thoroughly. Mix the milk with the liquid in which the marrow was cooked and gradually add the marrow and egg mixture. Reheat but do not boil. Season to taste.

Cream of Marrow Soup

1½ lb. cored, peeled marrow	*1 onion*
½ oz. butter	*2 sticks celery*
1 lump sugar	*1 pint milk*
Some chopped parsley	*Pepper and salt to taste*
1 pint water	

Cut the marrow into pieces. Slice celery and onion. Place in a pan and add water. Cover and cook until tender. Strain. Mash and rub marrow through a sieve. Return to pan and stir in the hot milk, butter and pepper and salt. Bring to the boil. Add sugar and parsley. Serve at once.

Marrow Salad

Cold cooked vegetable marrow, finely sliced, makes a pleasing addition to a vegetable or fish salad.

Marrow and Cheese Pie

1 marrow	*2 oz. margarine or butter*
2 oz. cheese	*Pepper and salt*

Cook the marrow in the usual way, and when tender drain and season with salt and pepper. Place a layer of marrow in the bottom of a greased fireproof dish, followed by a layer of grated cheese. Continue this until the dish is full—putting a layer of cheese on top. Place some dabs of margarine or butter over, and bake in a hot oven until nicely browned. A few fine breadcrumbs on the top give a nice finish to this dish.

Marrow Stew

1 medium-sized marrow	*1 teaspoonful sugar*
1 oz. margarine or butter	*4 tomatoes*
2 onions	*Pepper and salt*
½ pint water	

Peel the marrow and remove the seeds. Cut into small cubes and place in a saucepan with the skinned tomatoes and the sliced onions. Add the water, fat, sugar, and salt and pepper to season. Stew slowly for 1½ hours and serve with toast.

Stuffed Marrow

1 marrow	*1 oz. margarine or dripping*
¼ lb. chopped meat or fish	*1 onion*
1 egg	*1 tablespoonful milk*
Brown sauce or thick gravy	*1 oz. breadcrumbs*

Peel the marrow, cut off one end, and scoop out the seeds. Mix the meat with the breadcrumbs, milk, beaten egg, seasoning, and chopped onion. Put into a greased fireproof dish, cover, and bake slowly until tender; serve with the brown sauce or gravy.

Casserole of Marrow

1 medium-sized marrow	*2 tablespoonful butter*
1 lb. tomatoes	*2 medium-sized onions*
4 heaped tablespoonful grated cheese	*Pepper and salt to taste*

Choose a marrow 2–3 lb. in weight. Wash and cut, without peeling, into ¼ in. thick slices. Peel and chop the onions. Melt the butter in a saucepan. Add the onions, frying slowly. Stir frequently until clear and golden brown. Drain off butter into another frying pan. Add the marrow, and cook over a low heat, stirring frequently for five minutes. Add the tomatoes, salt and pepper to taste, and cover. Simmer for five minutes. Add the onion. Turn into a greased casserole. Cover and bake in a moderate oven for fifteen minutes, then sprinkle with grated cheese. Uncover and cook until brown on top. Use a shallow casserole or fireproof dish and choose a cheese with a strong taste.

Fruit Marrow

1 lb. apples	*1 small lemon*
1 lb. marrow	*Sugar*
2 oz. sultanas or raisins	*Pastry*

Peel the marrow and remove the seeds. Cut into small dice. Peel the apples and slice them. Fill a greased fireproof dish with alternate layers of marrow, apples and sultanas or raisins, sprinkling each layer liberally with sugar and a little lemon-rind or some drops of lemon juice. Add four teaspoonsful of water and cover with pastry. This can be eaten either hot or cold.

CHAPTER FOURTEEN

Salads and Herbs

It is always necessary to be able to produce palatable food, and the growing of a few herbs for the purpose of flavouring cannot be considered a waste of space. Correct seasoning can make a dish very appetizing, even though it is not the normal fare of the consumer. There is no need to grow more than three or four herbs as a rule, and this chapter, therefore, concentrates on these. They are all of them quite easy to cultivate, and can be used all the year round.

Salads, too, are useful because they are eaten fresh, and so are rich in vitamin content. Lettuce, for instance, is very high in vitamin A and C, quite high in vitamin B1, and contains vitamin B2 as well. It is true that the lettuce contains 95 per cent water, but even that is less than the marrow, and about the same as the runner bean and the onion. It does, however, contain 2 per cent carbohydrates and, in these, is equal to celery, radish and perpetual spinach, and is richer than the onion and cucumber.

Lettuce, too, contains lime and iron, which are necessary to balance the excess phosphates found in cereal and meat foods.

Even mustard and cress are useful, for their calorific content per pound stands at 125! Tomatoes are very useful indeed, since they are rich in vitamins.

CHIVES

This has been described as a baby salad onion. It grows in
a little clump, the clump spreading as the year proceeds.
Chives can be pulled or cut at any time of the year, and they
make it possible to have the subtle onion flavouring all the
year round.

The plants make a very nice edging to a border, and when
growing look something like thrift. They will do well under
quite dry conditions.

Propagation is effected by division in the spring.

LETTUCE

It is possible, by careful management and by the use of
continuous cloches or Access Frames, to ensure having crisp
hearts of lettuce all the year round.

Two groups are grown, the cos and the cabbage, but for
over-wintering, the cabbage type is to be preferred.

Lettuces can be cooked as well as eaten raw, and this is a
useful way of using up any that are starting to go to seed, or
which for some other reason are not fit for salad purposes.
The leaves and hearts should be boiled in a little water until
tender. This takes about 40 minutes. The water should then
be drained off, the leaves chopped up roughly, and returned
to the pan, plus a little margarine or butter and gravy, or a
few drops of meat extract.

Soil and Manuring When preparing the soil for lettuce,
much finely divided organic matter, such as sedge peat,
should be forked into the top 2 in. or so. This helps to ensure
that moisture is retained during the warmer months.
Powdery composted vegetable refuse may be used instead at
the rate of one good barrowload to 8 sq. yds.

Into the top 2 in. should be raked 2 oz. of a good fish
manure, ½ oz. precipitated bone phosphates, and 6 oz. of
wood ashes; all per square yard.

Seed Sowing The man who wishes to have lettuce all the year round should be prepared to sow a thimbleful of lettuce seed once every 3 weeks throughout the spring and summer, right up to the end of August.

The plants raised from these sowings may either be allowed to grow where they are sown, or may be thinned out and transplanted to further borders. The secret of success with lettuce transplanting is to do it when they are just big enough to handle.

The drills for the earliest sowings are usually 8 in. apart, and as soon as the young seedlings appear, they are thinned out to 2 in. apart. The sowings that are made in the open for growing where they are sown should be in rows 18 in. apart, the plants being thinned to 10 in. apart.

During the third week in August in the South, and about the second week in the North, seed should be sown on a warm seed bed, and the plants thus raised put out in rows 1 ft. apart and 10 in. apart in the rows. These are left outside to over-winter. Again, it is possible to sow the rows where the lettuces are to grow, and to thin the plants out to 5 in. before the winter sets in, and to 10 in. apart in the spring. They should be ready for use in May and early June.

Those who have Access Frames may make a sowing about the second week of October in the North, and the third week in the South, in rows 10 in. apart. The seedlings are thinned out to 9 in. apart, and the plants are left in the frames to winter, being given air on every possible occasion.

Lettuce seed may also be sown in November, the compost being a light one and rich in organic matter. The soil in which the lettuces are sown should be thoroughly soaked after seed sowing, and if this is done there should be no need to water after the plants are through.

Those who have cloches or Access Frames will find them particularly valuable for sowings made during the middle of August or the middle of October, for it is possible by using them to obtain lettuces up to the end of the year in the case of August sowings, and for an early spring supply in the case of those sown in October.

It is unnecessary to cover lettuce with cloches in the

summer, but they are of great value from mid-August onwards. The rows should run East and West, and then the sun's rays strike the glass at a right angle and therefore have greater powers of penetration.

Transplanting   As has already been said, lettuces should be transplanted early and firmly. They should be handled carefully, for they are tender and easily damaged. They should be transplanted quickly, for their roots soon dry out, but they should not be planted too deep as this makes them go 'peaky'.

General Cultivation   Keep down any weeds that appear. It is not advisable to go on the land in the winter if the soil is wet, but whenever the soil is warm enough, surface cultivation will do a great deal of good.

Cos lettuces do not heart as easily as cabbage varieties, and for this reason they are often tied round the middle with raffia when they have made three-quarters of their growth. Cos lettuces, too, seem to need far more moisture, and so should be watered regularly if the season is a dry one. It is usual only to make spring and summer sowings of the cos varieties.

Varieties

Cabbage—Spring Sowing
All the Year Round: a good variety for a hot summer. It will stand a good time before going to seed.
Wonderful: the curly, crinkly-leaved lettuce, much liked for its crispness.
Cluseed Borough Wonder: a large-hearted, first-class summer cabbage.

August Sowing
Arctic King: good for the North, for it survives a hard winter better than any other.
Imperial: produces large heads; is really hardy.

Improved Trocadero: produces solid attractive heads; is hardy and compact.

Cloche or Ganwick Culture
September and October sowings: Cheshunt Early Giant.
January and February sowings: Attractie.
March and April sowings: Suzan; All the Year Round.

Cos—Summer Sowing
Giant Perfection: an enormous heart.
Superb Folding White.
Lobjoit's Green Cos: good for late summer cutting. Has very broad foliage.

Winter Sowing
Winter Density: a dark green semi-cos, long standing and very hardy.

MUSTARD AND CRESS

One of the most easily grown crops, though on certain soils it 'damps off' easily. In such cases the soil may be watered with boiling water an hour before sowing.

Cress should be sown three days before mustard. It is usually convenient to sow in boxes, and these should be kept in the dark for a few days to ensure long stems. They should be brought out into the light again five days before cutting, to get the green colouring-matter back into the leaves.

Mustard and cress is cut off with scissors when required, as pulling up by the roots is apt to make the salad gritty.

The best variety for sowing is the white mustard. After the middle of March, mustard and cress may be sown outside, first of all in a South border, and then in a North border. Successive sowings may be made until the middle of September.

Rape is often used instead of mustard because the flavour is preferred.

8 As cress takes longer to grow than mustard, it should be sown three
days earlier.

RADISHES

With the introduction of new varieties the old idea about
indigestion does not hold good! They are one of the quickest
vegetables to grow. The seed is cheap and gives a big return.

Soil and Manuring Radishes do not need deep soil. They
will grow equally well on clays and sands, providing they are

properly prepared. The main thing is to see that the soil is not lumpy and that it is rich in organic matter. 2 oz. of fish manure, ½ oz. precipitated bone meal and 8 oz. of wood ashes should be raked into the top 2 in.

Seed Sowing   Radish seed should always be sown thinly. Broadcasting is possible, but it is better to sow in rows 6 in. apart, the drills being ½ in. deep.

The soil should always be made firm after sowing, as this ensures firm crisp radishes.

It is possible to make a sowing outside as late as December in a special sheltered place. The bed should be a raised one. After sowing, the bed should be covered with straw to a depth of 4 in., but immediately the seed has germinated the straw should be taken off, so as to allow the plants to grow in the light. If there is any sign of frost or snow, the straw should be replaced to give protection. It may be removed when the weather is warm.

The next sowing should be in a warm, dry border in February, this being covered with litter as before.

Further sowings may be made once a fortnight or every three weeks from the middle of March to the beginning of September. The summer sowings prefer a cool, shady place.

Radishes are a very useful crop, for they can be grown as an intercrop between the rows of other vegetables, such as peas, beans, carrots etc. They may also be sown in the rows of vegetables like parsnips and seakale, whose seeds take a long time to germinate.

Varieties

Round
Scarlet Globe: delicious flavour, good size and yet not coarse.
Cherry Belle: bright red, flesh white.

Oval
French Breakfast: deep crimson with white flesh inside. The root is solid and sweet.

Long

Wood's Frame: a firm scarlet early.

Icicle: a handsome, crisp white.

RADISHES—WINTER

Few people know about the excellent winter radishes. They grow large, and look more like turnips. They can be used in salads, or may be boiled and used as a vegetable. The roots may be left in the ground and dug up as desired.

Seed Sowing The seed should be sown in July in the North, and August in the South. The drills should be 9 in. apart, and when the plants are 2 in. high they should be thinned out to 6 in. apart.

Varieties

China Rose: bright rose; crisp, white flesh.

TOMATOES

Tomatoes can be grown in the open as well as under cloches or in glass-houses or Access Frames. In the open they are excellent grown against a South wall, and in fact in any sunny situation. They need plenty of air circulating around them.

Soil and Manuring If there is any fear that the soil is badly drained, the tomatoes should be planted on ridges with the farmyard manure below. Properly composted organic matter should be added, and in addition a good fish manure with a 10 per cent potash content should be forked into the top 3–4 in. During dry seasons a liquid manure may be used once a fortnight from July onwards. During wet seasons it helps if wood ashes can be applied at 4 oz. per sq. yd. late in June and late in July.

Seed Sowing   Those who have no greenhouse will be well advised to purchase sturdy, short-jointed plants about 8 in. high. These may be put in the ground about the end of May or the beginning of June.

Planting   The hole should not be too deep, and the gardener's aim should be to bury the roots so that they are covered with $\frac{1}{2}$ in. of new soil. Firm planting is essential, and, to prevent the plants from being damaged, they should be staked immediately with a bamboo.

Where a number of plants are to be grown in a row, two strong posts should be put at each end and a wire stretched tightly between them. The plants can then be tied up to the wires where they are to go.

General Cultivation   Directly the plants are in, sedge peat should be applied over the surface of the soil as a mulch.

Side shoots should be removed as they grow so as to restrict the plants to one or two main stems. As a new growth takes place, so must tying be attended to, and, when tying, a space should be left for the stem to swell.

During the first week of August it is advisable to stop the plants—that is, to pinch off the growing point. Large numbers of side shoots will push out as a result of the stopping, and these must be removed immediately.

In order to allow the sun to get at the ripening fruit, whole leaves may be removed here and there right back to the main stem. It is better to do this than to cut back a large number of leaves by half.

Spraying as a preventive against the potato blight may be necessary in wet years, as advised for potatoes.

Harvesting   The fruit should be picked as it ripens. It is fairly easy to continue the ripening of the fruit indoors, if necessary, on the window-ledge. Any fruits that have not ripened by the end of September must be removed and ripened in the house.

Varieties The best varieties for outside growing are:

Amateur Improved: an extremely dwarf variety, height 15–18 in., fruit of excellent quality and flavour; does not need staking.

Easicrop: a dwarf which ripens a little earlier than Amateur; excellent for sandwiches.

Unwins Histon Early: a good early variety of first-class quality and flavour.

Outdoor Girl: produces very heavy crops of well-flavoured, slightly oval fruits.

Histon Cropper: small compact plants with little foliage, produces ripe fruit often earlier than other varieties. Highly resistant to blight.

WATER-CRESS

Few people realize that water-cress can be grown without water, and as it is one of the most valuable salads, it should certainly be more widely grown.

A water-cress bed can be made almost any time in the spring. A shady situation is best, and a dark, damp corner where nothing else will grow is ideal.

A simple plan is to dig a trench 1 ft. deep and 2 ft. wide, and place in the bottom of it a 6 in. layer of well rotted and prepared compost. This should be given a thorough soaking, and the trench should be left for 14 days or so, two or three bucketsful of water being poured into the trench every day.

Before planting, 2 in. of good garden soil should be placed over the compost and pressed firm. The young plants should be set out 8 in. square in this.

If seed is to be sown directly into the trench, three or four seeds may be sown at each 'station' 8 in. apart, the seedlings being thinned down to one or two if they all germinate.

During germination the trench should be kept dark by covering it with old sacks or matting laid across a framework of bamboos or poles.

The soil should never be allowed to get dry, and should be watered every day through a fine rose, unless it rains. When the young plants are rooted, the leading shoots should be pinched out, and the plants will thus bush out. Later, if there is any sign of the plants flowering, they should be cut back and allowed to start again.

In order to keep up a constant supply of young plants, it is better to make three or four small beds rather than one large one. The stems that are pulled off are thus fresher and more palatable.

The hard work concerned with growing water-cress is the regular watering.

HERBS

Mint

The Spearmint and Apple Mint are the two varieties which are most used for mint sauce. They are propagated by means of division of roots. The roots may be cut up into pieces an inch long, and these can be planted 6 in. apart in any suitable situation. Mint will grow almost anywhere.

A damp situation is best, and to ensure freedom from rust and the maximum crop, a new bed should be made in March each year.

Where rust is very bad the roots should be washed before planting, or they may be put in warm water at a temperature of 110°F for twenty minutes. After washing, the underground stems should be trimmed so as to remove the little roots.

Use both the mints together to make the best mint sauce.

Parsley

Parsley makes a good edging plant. It should always be sown thinly if good rows are to result. Thinning should be carried out early to prevent the plants from crowding.

9 Pouring boiling water over newly sown parsley seed helps it to germinate. Cut parsley with a long stalk.

Parsley will grow in almost any soil. A sowing may be made in March for the summer and in June for the winter. If only one sowing is to be made, this is best done in May. Water the drill with boiling water after the seed is sown.

If one or two rows are to be sown, they should be 1 ft. apart. In all cases the plants should be thinned out first of all to 3 in. apart, and finally to 6 in. apart. The thinnings may be transplanted to other rows if necessary.

If the plants tend to get coarse, they should be cut down and the young growth that results will be green and tender.

Sage

The broad-leaved green sage is the most valuable. It is better to buy plants than to sow seed. Cuttings may be taken with a piece of the older wood attached in April or May, and may be rooted in a sandy medium.

The plants should be put out in rows 2 ft. apart and 1 ft. apart in the rows. After planting they should be hoed regularly and if they show signs of flowering, the flowering stems should be removed.

Thyme

Either the common thyme or the lemon thyme may be grown. Both make an effective edging and can be used in dry borders where parsley will not grow readily. The common thyme may be raised from seed sowings, but it is better to propagate the lemon thyme by division of roots in March and April, or by cuttings in September.

The rows should be 2 ft. apart, and the plants 18 in. apart in the rows.

CHAPTER FIFTEEN

Salad-Making and Herb-Drying

In the chapters dealing with the various vegetables, an endeavour has been made in each instance to give some advice about salads. This chapter, therefore, deals with salads and saladings as a whole, and gives some special recipes which for various reasons have not been included in the other chapters.

Many of the recipes are for mixed salads which could not legitimately appear under the heading of one particular vegetable.

Salads are rich in vitamins. Lettuce, for instance, is rich in vitamin C, quite rich in vitamin B1, and contains vitamin B2 as well. Lettuce not only contains 2 per cent carbohydrate, but also lime and iron, which are so necessary to balance the excess of phosphates found in cereal and meat foods.

Even the humble mustard and cress are useful, for their calorific content per pound stands as high as 125, and their carbohydrate content at 4 per cent. No one doubts the value of the tomato, which is rich in vitamins A, B1, B2 and C; and contains 4 per cent carbohydrates as well.

At the end of the chapter will be found some recipes for salad dressings.

GENERAL RULES FOR SALAD-MAKING

1. Remember that there are far more vegetables than can be used for salads than you have thought of in the past!
2. You can use many of the vegetables, either in their raw state or cooked; shredded cabbage, shredded carrots, shredded artichokes, etc., are all excellent raw. Peas, beans, cauliflower, and so on, can be used raw as well as cooked.
3. Keep the different constituents of a salad separate; clean them separately, etc., until the time comes actually to mix them together.
4. Always wash the fresh saladings, such as lettuce, endive, chicory, sorrel, water-cress, etc. in very cold, clean water, so as to crisp them up. Dry them afterwards in a cloth, or, better still, put them in a wire salad-basket and whirl them round and round in the open to get rid of the moisture.
5. It is always better to shred vegetables with your fingers if possible. If this is not easy, use a silver knife.
6. Celeriac will always supply the necessary celery flavour, and so will the centre white heart of a large cabbage if sprinkled with celery salt.
7. If you prefer your tomatoes without their skins, dip them in boiling water for a minute, when the skins will come off easily without softening the centres.
8. It is convenient sometimes to serve the salad without covering it with salad dressing, so that those at the meal may use as much dressing as they desire. If you are very particular, serve one or two alternative dressings for your guests to use.

Salad of Cooked Vegetables

1 teacupful cooked French beans
1 teacupful cooked peas
1 teaspoonful finely chopped chives or the green part of spring onions
1 teacupful cooked asparagus points
1 teacupful young, cooked carrots
Salad dressing

The vegetables should be cooked separately, and the beans cut not too finely. Merely take off the ends and edges. The carrots should be thinly sliced. Allow the vegetables to become quite cold, and then arrange them tastefully in a salad bowl. Pour over the salad dressing and decorate with the chopped chives or spring onions. The above vegetables are suggestions, but any suitable cooked vegetables may be utilized in the same way.

A Simple Salad

2 medium-sized lettuces	½ teaspoonful castor sugar
½ lb. tomatoes	Salad dressing

Wash and prepare the lettuce, skin the tomatoes by dipping them in boiling water and peeling with a sharp knife. Slice them when they have become quite cold. Dry the lettuce carefully. Moisten it, and the tomato, with a salad dressing and place in a salad bowl. Half a teaspoonful of castor sugar makes a pleasant addition to the dressing.

Potato Salad

1 tablespoonful chopped gherkin	1 teaspoonful French mustard
6 potatoes	1 teacupful chopped celery
3 tablespoonsful mayonnaise	2 tablespoonsful chopped
1 tablespoonful vinegar	pimento
	1 onion

Cook the potatoes in their skins in salted water. When cool, peel and slice them. Mix with the onion, which should be finely chopped, and the celery and pimento. Season with pepper and salt to taste. Stir in the mayonnaise, vinegar, mustard, and the gherkin.

A Summer Salad

1 lettuce	Radishes
3 tomatoes	1 hard-boiled egg
Small cucumber	Spring onions
1 small beetroot	Salad dressing

Prepare the lettuce and shred it. Peel the tomatoes and slice them. Peel and slice the beetroot and cucumber, and prepare the radishes. Place half the ingredients in a salad bowl, and use the remainder for garnishing. Serve with a good salad dressing.

A Winter Salad

1 cooked beetroot	*2 cooked potatoes*
2 cooked carrots	*1 small carrot*
1 bunch water-cress	*1 stick celery*
6 walnuts	*Salad dressing*

Wash and prepare the water-cress and celery. Wash, peel, and grate the small carrot. Cut the cooked vegetables into dice, and the walnuts in halves. Place in a salad bowl and pour the dressing over. Decorate with the raw carrot and fancy-shaped cuttings of beetroot.

Russian Salad

2 tablespoonsful cooked peas	*2 gherkins*
1 tablespoonful cooked carrot	*1 tablespoonful cooked potato*
1 tablespoonful French beans	*5 or 6 capers*
Few pieces cooked cauliflower	

Dice the vegetables where possible, chop the capers and place all in a salad bowl in layers, putting a little dressing between each layer. Finish off the top with a thicker layer of dressing and decorate with shaped pieces of vegetable.

Chinese Salad

2 apples	*2 tomatoes*
1 banana	*Small piece cucumber*
6 pineapple chunks	*6 lettuce leaves*
2 cooked potatoes	*Salad dressing*
6 walnuts	

Prepare all ingredients and place in a salad bowl. The pineapple should be cut into small dice and the walnuts halved.

The other ingredients should be diced or sliced. Garnish the top with salad dressing and pineapple strips.

Tomato Salad (i)

6 good firm tomatoes	1 teaspoonful chopped parsley
1 onion	Salad dressing

Skin and slice the tomatoes and chop the onion finely. Arrange the tomatoes in a salad bowl and sprinkle the grated onion over. Pour over the salad dressing, and garnish with the chopped parsley.

Tomato Salad (ii)

1 lb. tomatoes	1 small onion
1 tablespoonful vinegar	¼ teaspoonful salt
Juice of 1 lemon	½ teaspoonful castor sugar
1 oz. grated cheese	Pepper

Skin the tomatoes. Put them in a salad bowl and sprinkle with chopped onion. To the vinegar add the lemon juice, sugar, salt and pepper. Pour this over the tomatoes and serve with grated cheese.

Celery, Walnut and Beetroot Salad

1 beetroot	6 walnuts
2 sticks of white celery	French dressing

Dice the beetroot, cut the celery into small pieces and the walnuts into quarters. Cover with salad or French dressing and decorate the top with a few pieces of beetroot.

Cheese and Tomato Salad

2 small lettuces	1 hard-boiled egg
2 oz. cheese	3 tomatoes

Wash the lettuce and skin the tomatoes. Grate the cheese and chop the hard-boiled egg. Break up the lettuce. Mix well and place in a salad bowl. Serve with salad dressing.

Roman Salad

2 lettuces	1 onion
½ teaspoonful honey	1 tablespoonful vinegar

Wash and dry the lettuce and break into small pieces. Sweeten the vinegar with the honey and mix in the chopped onion. Pour over the lettuce, and serve with dressing if preferred.

Pea and Bean Salad

½ teaspoonful chopped parsley	½ lb. cooked French beans
1 lb. cooked green peas	1 hard-boiled egg
1 small beetroot	Salad dressing

Mix the peas and beans with a tablespoonful of salad dressing and garnish with the beetroot cut into dice, and the egg cut into thin rings. Sprinkle the top with chopped parsley.

Surprise Salad

1 head of celery	Small bunch water-cress
1 oz. shelled nuts	1 banana

Wash the water-cress in salted water and pick off all white threads, brown leaves, etc. Peel the banana and cut into thin slices. Wash and trim the celery and cut into small pieces. Chop the nuts coarsely. Mix all ingredients well together and serve with a good salad dressing.

Apple, Nut and Celery Salad

6 apples	Mayonnaise sauce
1 small lettuce	2 oz. chopped walnuts
1 stick celery	Pepper and salt

Choose nice, smooth, rosy apples and polish them well. Cut off the tops and remove the insides. Wash and chop the lettuce, celery and nuts, and add the pepper and salt. Thoroughly mix in the mayonnaise, and put the mixture into the apple-cases, piling well up on top. Decorate with small celery leaves.

Cabbage Salad

Celery—a few sticks   1 banana
cabbage leaves   1 apple

Wash some crisp, fresh cabbage leaves and shred them finely. Peel and chop the apple, banana and celery. Mix with two tablespoonsful of mayonnaise and pile in a salad bowl, or glass dish, decorating with cream cheese or chopped nuts.

Lettuce and Green-Pea Salad

2 medium-sized lettuces   Mayonnaise or French dressing
2 tomatoes   Pepper and salt
1 lb. cooked green peas

Wash the lettuce and pull the leaves apart separately. Into each leaf place a spoonful of peas, and place a slice of tomato (previously skinned by putting into boiling water and peeling with a sharp knife) on the top. Season with pepper and salt and serve with mayonnaise or French dressing.

Tomato and Celery Salad

6 ripe tomatoes   Salad dressing
1 small onion   Pepper and salt
1 stick celery

Peel the tomatoes and slice them thinly. Wash the celery and cut into thin strips. Chop the onion finely and mix all the ingredients together, seasoning with pepper and salt. Serve with a good salad dressing.

SALAD DRESSINGS

French Dressing

2 tablespoonsful vinegar   Juice of ½ lemon
6–8 tablespoonsful olive oil   ½ teaspoonful mustard
Sugar to taste   Pepper
½ teaspoonful salt

Mix the mustard, sugar, salt and pepper together, and then add the oil gradually, also the lemon juice. Then add the vinegar and mix thoroughly.

Mayonnaise

> *Yolks of 2 eggs*   *Vinegar*
> *1 cupful salad oil*   *Pepper and salt*
> *¼ teaspoonful mustard*

Mix the salt, pepper and mustard, and add to the egg yolks. Stir with a wooden spoon, adding the oil drop by drop until the sauce is the consistency of very thick cream. Then add vinegar to taste. Be sure to keep the utensils and the ingredients very cold while preparing, or the mixture may curdle.

Eggless Mayonnaise

> *1 teaspoonful icing sugar*   *1 teaspoonful salt*
> *1 teaspoonful mustard*   *1 small baked potato*
> *¾ cupful olive oil*   *Little vinegar*

Peel and mash the potato. Stir in the icing sugar, mustard and salt. Gradually add the vinegar and rub the mixture through a fine sieve. Add the oil slowly and mix well.

Salad Cream

> *1 egg*   *1 teaspoonful dry mustard*
> *1 teaspoonful sugar*   *½ pint vinegar*
> *½ pint milk*   *1½ teaspoonsful flour*
> *½ oz. butter or margarine*   *1 teaspoonful salt*

Beat the egg thoroughly. Mix the dry ingredients together well and add the egg. Put into a pan, adding the butter or margarine, and cook over a low heat until thickened. Stir all the time. This usually takes about fifteen minutes. This sauce can be bottled and kept for three or four weeks.

THE DRYING OF HERBS

It is comparatively easy to dry herbs, and all housewives should prepare their own mint, sage, thyme, parsley, marjoram, etc. The leaves should be gathered when the plants are about to flower as they are then at their best. The picking should be done in the morning, just after the dew has gone and before the sun is too hot, and on a dry day.

Herbs with very small leaves, like thyme, should be thoroughly washed while still on their stems, and should then be tied in bunches and hung up in the kitchen to dry. They are best placed into a butter-muslin bag, so as to prevent them from becoming dusty.

When dry, it is quite easy to strip the leaves off the stems, for they should then be quite crisp. The crushing may be completed by rolling with a rolling-pin, or by sieving them through a wire sieve.

The herbs with larger leaves, like parsley and mint, should be picked off the stalks and washed. They should then be tied up in a length of butter-muslin and dipped into the boiling bicarbonate of soda solution (usual formula $\frac{1}{4}$ oz. to 2 quarts water). This dipping preserves their colour. After blanching, drain for a few minutes and then spread the leaves on the muslin-covered tray and place in a cool oven or in front of the kitchen stove at a temperature of about 120°F. It should be possible, if this temperature is constant, to prepare them in an hour. Placed above a kitchen stove they often take three or four hours.

When crisp and dry they should be crushed to powder as advised for thyme, and should then be stored, wrapped in grease-proof paper and covered with dark paper, to prevent the light getting at them. It is possible to keep parsley for months and still retain its lovely green colour.

The herbs may either be stored separately or can be mixed together. A good mixture for ordinary kitchen use consists of 1 part thyme, 1 part winter savoury, 1 part sweet marjoram and 2 parts parsley. The parts are, of course, by weight.

Other leaves and seeds which may be dried in a similar

manner are the leaves of the bay tree, tarragon for making tarragon vinegar, dill for use in pickles, and nasturtium seeds which are an excellent substitute for capers. After the seeds are dry they should be stored in white vinegar, adding to each half-pint used 1 bay leaf, $\frac{1}{4}$ oz. salt and 3 peppercorns.

CHAPTER SIXTEEN

The Unusual is Helpful

There are a number of unusual vegetables rich in vitamins and high in calorific value. They are no more difficult to grow than the ordinary kinds, and they do provide an important appetising change from the eternal potatoes and cabbage.

CELERIAC

This grows like a turnip and tastes just like the heart of celery. It is excellent when sliced into salad or when cooked. It is easy to grow, and has not got to be earthed-up or blanched like celery. Another great advantage is that the vegetable will keep for six months after it is fully grown.

The seed should be sown as for self-blanching celery, the seedlings being pricked out into frames when large enough. The young plants should be put out in May or early June in rows 12 in. apart, the plants being 12 in. apart in the rows. When planting, the side-growths should be removed.

Celeriac is a gross feeder, and should be grown on land that has been well manured. One good barrowload of properly composted vegetable refuse may be forked into 8 sq. yds. In addition a good fish manure should be forked into the top 3 in. at 4 oz. to the sq. yd.

The rows should be kept free from weeds and, if possible,

should be watered once a week from the end of June onwards. Bottled liquid manure, such as Farmura, may be added to each watering if the land is poor.

A fortnight before the roots are to be lifted, sedge peat should be applied over the roots up to the foliage to cause the upper part to become blanched. The celeriac may be dug up and stored in soil in a shed, or in a clamp as advised for potatoes. In the South of England it is possible to leave the roots outside and cover them up during very hard frosts with soil or bracken.

SQUASHES

These form a very valuable food, for, after harvesting, the large, marrow-like fruits may be stored in a shed, and portions may be cut off as desired for use throughout the winter. They should be grown in the same way as marrows, either being made to climb up wire-netting or a fence, or being grown on the rubbish-heap or on the flat.

The plants should be raised in frames or under glass from seed sown in pots any time during April or early May. Two seeds are usually sown per 3 in. pot, and if both grow, the weakest is removed.

It is possible, also, to sow the seeds where the plants are to grow, but this results in later cropping.

Slugs are partial to these plants, and should be kept at bay by the use of Draza pellets.

Any old fermenting compost may be buried in a heap so as to give the young plants a hot-bed underneath. This heating of the soil gets them growing quickly from the start.

The squashes may be harvested directly they are of sufficient size, or they can be left until they are full grown, so that they may be hung up for use during the winter.

Varieties

Hubbard Squash: should not be eaten until September or October. Will keep until February. Perhaps the most useful

10 Squash seeds are sown two to a pot. If both grow, the weaker one
is discarded. They can be trained up a fence. After harvesting,
winter varieties are hung up in a shed and portions can be cut off
and used as desired.

winter variety. Should be steamed, or the pieces baked in
their own skin, and then mashed with butter. Makes a
delicious soup when made up with milk, and also a
delicious pie.

Banana Squash: has the consistency of a banana, with a
delicious flavour. It is a summer variety.

Acorn Squash: a small variety. Should be cooked whole, one being served to each person. Is lovely stuffed with meat or ham.

Golden Scallop Squash: is quite round and is excellent served with bacon in the morning. Can be kept for use all the year round. Is first-class for the winter months.

PUMPKINS

These may be grown in exactly the same way as squashes or marrows. They are very useful because they keep and have a flavour of their own.

MARROW, PUMPKIN AND SQUASH TIPS

It is sometimes necessary to pinch back the growing tips of marrows, pumpkins, or squashes, and these should be saved and used in the kitchen, for they form an excellent substitute for spinach.

If marrows are grown in rows, it is often advisable to keep them pinched back, and when this is done a dual-purpose vegetable is produced.

KOHL RABI

Kohl Rabi is a very popular vegetable on the Continent. It is similar in flavour to the turnip, but is more 'nutty'. Its great advantage is that it will stand quite hard frosts, and so may be left growing in the ground until required. Furthermore, it is not so liable to club root disease as the turnip, and so may be used on disease-infected land.

The seed may be sown any time from the second week of March until the second week of August. Those who want continuity may make a succession of sowings every three weeks. The rows should be 2 ft. apart, and the seedlings thinned to 3 in. apart in the early stages, and finally to 6 in.

apart. The young plants pulled at this final thinning are in a fit condition to be used as a vegetable. Thus this method of thinning is important.

When hoeing, the earth should not be drawn up to the plants, but rather away from them.

Varieties

For early work: Earliest White: delicately flavoured.
For later sowings: Early Green: a winter vegetable.

SUGAR PEA

An excellent pea, eaten pod and all! There is no need to do any shelling, and the pod has a definite food value. It is advisable just to top and tail, like gooseberries, before boiling them.

The seed should be sown in exactly the same way as for ordinary peas, the main sowing being made in May, in rows 4 ft. apart. It grows to a height of 5 or 6 ft. and requires the support of pea sticks or wire-netting.

The pods should be picked regularly while they are young and fresh. If any of the pods are allowed to get old, the plant ceases to crop heavily.

SALSIFY

A root crop which is becoming increasingly popular, even though it is still classed as 'unusual'.

It grows best on a light, loamy soil, though it will do quite well in a heavy clay, providing it has been properly prepared. It does best, perhaps, when following a crop that has been well manured the previous year. Like other root crops, it should not be grown on soil that has been recently manured with farmyard manure. Fertilizers should be applied as advised for parsnips.

The seed should be sown in April, the drills being 12 in.

apart and 1 in. deep. Directly the seedlings are large enough they should be thinned out, first of all to 4 in. apart, and then to 8 in. apart.

Keep down weeds and apply sedge peat or powdery compost alongside the rows to prevent annual weeds. The roots should never be cut when working among them, or they tend to bleed.

It should be possible to use the roots first of all during the second or third week of October, but, like parsnips, they come to no harm if left in the ground until required. They therefore need take up little storage room—a good point in their favour.

The best variety is Mammoth Sandwich Island.

CHAPTER SEVENTEEN

Unusual Vegetable Recipes

Men often complain to the author that the reason they do not grow unusual vegetables is that their wives have no idea how to cook them. This chapter deals only with the unusual vegetables that are mentioned in the previous chapter. There is nothing difficult about growing the vegetables, nor should there be any difficulty in cooking them.

CELERIAC

Boiled Celeriac

The roots should be peeled thinly, quartered, and placed in boiling salted water in a saucepan. They should then be boiled until tender, and be served covered with a thick white sauce.

Some prefer to boil them in a vegetable stock (this usually takes ninety minutes), and then to serve them with melted butter or margarine.

Celeriac Soup

The celeriac should be boiled, and, when cooked, ¼ lb. should be rubbed through a fine wire sieve. Add one teaspoonful of finely chopped onion. Stir and place in a saucepan, together with a cupful of milk and a tablespoonful of butter or margarine. Heat, and when almost boiling, stir in the yolk of an egg and a teaspoonful of finely chopped parsley. This soup should never be boiled. If it seems too thick, more milk can be added.

Browned Celeriac

Boil the vegetable well as before, take out of the saucepan when tender and cut up while still warm and place in a shallow fireproof dish. Pour on a little melted butter or margarine and grate sufficient cheese over the top (some people like more cheese, and some less). Put in a quick oven to brown. Serve garnished with finely chopped parsley.

SQUASHES

Squashes are a kind of gourd with the Latin name *Curcurbita pepo*. They are much grown in Canada and America, and they are becoming popular in this country. They grow exactly like a marrow, and either climb up wire netting or may be trained along a fence or grown on a rubbish-heap or on the flat. Their great advantage is that they can be stored in a shed, and portions may be cut off as desired for use throughout the winter. They form a very valuable food.

There are various kinds of squashes, and it is proposed, therefore, to treat each one individually.

Hubbard Squash

These should be used in September and October, and, if gathered before the frost touches them, can be stored in a cool, dry place until February. The flesh is something like that of the pumpkin, but has its own distinctive flavour. It should never be boiled. It must be steamed, or the pieces baked in their own skin and then mashed with margarine or butter and seasoned with a sprinkling of herbs and a little sugar.

Hubbard Squash Soup

Makes a delicious soup, made up with milk as advised for celeriac (see p. 189).

Hubbard Squash Pie

Should be made into a pie as advised for pumpkin (see p. 197). It has a delicious special flavour.

Note The Hubbard squashes grow in all kinds of colours—green, red, striped and warty-looking, but they all taste alike.

Banana Squash

This has the consistency of a banana, with a delicious flavour. It may be used as a vegetable or as a sweet.

Acorn Squash

These grow small and should be cooked whole, one being served to each person. They are lovely served as an entrée or as a savoury, stuffed with kidneys, chopped pork or ham.

Noodle Squash

After puncturing one end of this squash it should be steamed whole. It should then be cut in half and the contents turned out. This should be served hot with a little melted butter or margarine, seasoned with pepper and salt.

Noodle Squash Salad

After turning out, allow to cool. When cold, serve alone as a salad with mayonnaise dressing.

Golden Scallop Squash

This is a round squash and should be served with bacon in the morning. It is most extensively used in Canada and the United States, and can be obtained there all the year round.

Crookneck Squash Fried

Cut in slices and dip in seasoned flour. Fry in enough melted butter to cover the bottom of the pan, for about ten minutes, turning occasionally until tender and evenly browned. Drain on absorbent paper.

If preferred, egg and crumb the pieces after flouring, or substitute batter for flour and egg and crumbs, and fry in deep hot fat until golden. Drain on absorbent paper.

Scalloped Winter Squash

4 cups well mashed squash	½ cupful moistened breadcrumbs
1 oz. butter	1 egg well beaten
1 tablespoon onion well minced	Pepper and salt to taste
1 teaspoonful mixed herbs	

Wrap a medium-sized Butternut or Hubbard squash in aluminium foil. Bake in a fairly slow oven, say 325°F until tender. Halve lengthwise. Remove the seeds. Remove the pulp without breaking the shell. Melt some fat in a saucepan; add the onion. Fry slowly until slightly browned. Soak the bread in milk to cover for five minutes, then drain and mash. Add with the squash to the onion. Simmer gently for five minutes, stirring occasionally. Remove from the stove. Season with the pepper and salt and herbs. Stir in the egg. Pack into scallop shells, sprinkle with sieved stale breadcrumbs, fleck with the butter and bake until brown.

Provencale Squash

3 small squashes, size of tennis balls	½ oz. butter
	1½ tablespoonsful water
4 sliced, peeled tomatoes	1 teaspoonful salt
Grated Parmesan cheese to taste	Pepper to taste
1 teaspoonful crushed garlic	
5 dessertspoonsful olive oil	

Remove tops of squashes, then cut in slices 1 in. thick. Place garlic and one dessertspoonful oil in a small pan. Cook for one minute, then add to squashes. Cover and simmer gently until tender. Fry tomato slices for two minutes in remainder of oil, heated slightly. Add to the squash. Season with pepper and salt to taste, then transfer to a hot, shallow fireproof dish. Sprinkle with grated Parmesan cheese. Brown slightly under grill. Enough for four people.

Squash en Surprise

1½ cups mashed squash　　　*1½ tablespoonsful minced onion*
2 oz. salt pork　　　　　　*Pepper and salt to taste*
1 tablespoonful minced parsley

Dice the pork. Place the squash in a basin and add the parsley. Melt the fat trimmings from pork, then add the pork. Fry until lightly browned. Drain off half the fat and add onion to remainder. Cook for a few minutes, then divide pork between two hot plates. Heat squash with onion. Season to taste and serve on the pork. Sufficient for two people.

Squash Pancakes

1½ cups boiled squash sieved　　*1½ cups stale breadcrumbs*
2 tablespoonsful boiled　　　　*1 yolk of an egg*
*　　minced onion*　　　　　　*Pepper and salt to taste*
2 tablespoonsful Parmesan
*　　cheese grated*

Mix the squash with the onion and cheese. Stir in the crumbs, the egg yolk and the pepper and salt to taste. Turn into a saucepan and stir over low heat until mixture thickens. Remove and leave it to cool. With floured hands, shape into little cakes, about 3 in. across. Coat with egg and breadcrumbs and fry in a little smoking hot butter until brown below, then turn and brown on other side.

Squash Soufflé

1 cup squash mashed　　　　*1 cup thick white sauce*
1 tablespoonful grated shallot　*2 eggs*
2 tablespoonsful parsley minced　*Salt and paprika to taste*
1 tablespoonful melted butter

Separate the eggs. Beat all the other ingredients together except the egg whites. When blended beat egg whites to a stiff froth and fold into the mixture. Three-quarters fill buttered custard cups. Stand in a baking tin with hot water coming halfway up the sides. Bake in a moderate oven, say 350°F, until firm in the centre. Takes about twenty minutes. Remove from oven and stand for five minutes. Turn each on to a round of hot buttered toast. Cover with a nice cheese sauce.

Ring Squash

3 cups squash mashed	1½ oz. butter
1 tablespoonful onion grated well	Pepper and salt to taste
3 eggs well-beaten	

Steam the squash then mash or sieve. The 'mash' must be perfectly smooth. Stir in the remaining ingredients. Place in a greased round and stand in a baking tin with hot water coming halfway up sides. Bake in a moderate oven, say 350°F, until firm and golden. Takes about one hour. Turn out on to a hot dish. Fill the centre with creamed peas or cooked chicken pieces.

Sausage-Acorn Squash

1 small Acorn squash per person   1 lb. sausage meat per 4 persons

Cut the Acorn squashes in half. Place them cut-side down in a pan. Pour in boiling water to ¼ in. depth. Bake in moderate oven for twenty-five minutes. Turn squashes cut-sides up with fork. Fill centres with half-cooked sausage meat. Bake until tender—say twenty minutes.

Butter-Bean Squash

1 small Acorn squash per person	6 oz. butter
1 lb. dried butter beans	4 tablespoonsful chopped chives

Bake the halved squash (without any stuffing) in ¼ in. depth of water, as advised for Sausage-Acorns; remove when partially cooked. Meanwhile boil the butter beans in water and when soft, mash them up well and add butter and chives. Mix well. Fill in the upturned squash halves with the mashed beans and cook for another fifteen to twenty minutes in a moderate oven.

Crookneck Summer Squash

1 large squash	*¼ lb. butter*
2 oz. onion juice	*Pepper and salt*

Cut a large Crookneck summer squash in half lengthwise. Remove all the seeds. Hollow out some of the pulp. Dice the unprepared squash (i.e. the other half). Cook for ten minutes in a little water. Mix with a little salt, the butter, the onion juice and a generous sprinkling of pepper. Heap this into the hollowed out half. Bake for one hour in a moderate oven.

Squash and Marjoram

1 squash	*4 oz. butter*
4 oz. freshly chopped marjoram	

Remove the stem end. Cut in half lengthwise. Remove large seeds and coarse fibre, if any. Slice in pieces about 1 in. thick. Boil pieces for ten to fifteen minutes. Put in a warmed dish. Mix the marjoram with the melted butter and pour over the squash. Serve immediately.

The alternative is to mash the squash with the butter and marjoram, and put back into the moderate oven for another five minutes—and then serve.

Squash and Walnut Sweet Croquettes

2 cups boiled or steamed squash	*1 dessertspoonful castor sugar*
1 egg well beaten	*3 tablespoonsful flour*
2 tablespoonsful melted butter	*¼ teaspoonful salt*
1 third cupful chopped walnuts	

Mix all the ingredients together. Divide into small equal portions. Shape into egg shaped 'cakes' with slightly floured hands. Cover with egg and breadcrumbs and fry in deep hot fat until golden. Drain on absorbent paper. Should be sufficient for six people.

Stuffed Squash

3 medium-sized squashes	*3 chopped hard-boiled eggs*
½ cup parsley sauce	*1 cup grated cheese*
1 dessertspoonful onion grated	*½ cup stale breadcrumbs*
1½ tablespoonsful green pepper, chopped fine	*Pepper and salt to taste*

Boil the squashes for fifteen minutes until nearly tender, in salted water. Drain well. Scoop out the pulp, but leave shell about ¾ in. thick. Mash the pulp until smooth. Add the sauce, onion, pepper and eggs and half the cheese. When well mixed, fill shells. Sprinkle with breadcrumbs. Fleck with butter, then sprinkle with the remainder of the cheese. Place side by side in a baking tin containing a little water. Bake in a moderately hot oven, say 375°F, for half an hour until golden. Halve and serve. Should be sufficient for six people.

Mushroom Stuffing for Small Squashes

Several squashes	*1 teaspoonful shallot grated*
½ cup mushrooms cut up	*1 pinch crushed mixed herbs*
2 oz. butter	*1 beaten egg*
¾ cup breadcrumbs, preferably stale	*Pepper and salt to taste*

Halve the parboiled squashes. Melt the fat in a frying pan and add the mushrooms. Fry slowly until tender, then stir in remaining ingredients. Stuff and bake the squashes in a moderately hot oven, say 375°F, until the filling is set and lightly browned.

Other fillings you can use for small baked squashes are: creamed crab, sweetbreads, chicken, oysters, veal and green peas.

PUMPKINS

Boiled Pumpkin

Peel the pumpkin, cut into portions, remove the seeds, and boil in salted water for twenty minutes until tender. Drain in a colander, serve garnished with toast and covered with a thick white sauce.

Fried Pumpkin

Peel the pumpkin and remove the seeds. Steam (if possible). If not, boil until nearly tender. Drain thoroughly, keeping slices whole. Coat with batter or egg and breadcrumbs and fry in hot fat until brown.

Pumpkin Soup

2 lb. sliced pumpkin	*1 oz. butter or margarine*
Little grated nutmeg	*1 quart milk*
1 tablespoonful flour	*Pepper and salt*

The pumpkin should be peeled, the seeds removed, and, after slicing, should be thrown into boiling salted water and boiled until tender. Strain off the water and rub the vegetable through a fine sieve.

In another saucepan bring to boil slowly the quart of milk. Stir in the flour, a little at a time, and put in the butter or margarine. Grate a little nutmeg over the top, and add a saltspoonful of white pepper.

Add the pumpkin pulp by degrees, stirring thoroughly. If too thick, add a little more milk. Season with salt and serve hot.

Pumpkin Pie (i)

2 lb. peeled pumpkin	*2 tablespoonful sugar*
2 tablespoonful milk	*1 egg*
¼ teaspoonful grated lemon rind	*Pinch of ginger*
Pinch of cinnamon	*Pinch of salt*

Prepare the pumpkin as usual, removing the seeds, and boil in salted water until tender, afterwards passing the vegetable through a fine sieve. To this mixture add the egg, sugar, lemon rind, ginger, and cinnamon, and beat and stir well. Add the milk during beating. Put this mixture into a pie dish. Cover with pastry and bake in a moderate oven for forty minutes. Sufficient for four people.

Pumpkin Pie (ii)

1 pastry case 9 in. across	*Pinch of ground cloves*
½ lb. castor sugar	*3 well-beaten eggs*
½ teaspoonful ground cinnamon	*2 cups of milk*
¼ teaspoonful grated nutmeg	*2 cups sieved steamed pumpkin*
½ teaspoonful ground ginger	*¾ teaspoonful salt*

When making the pastry case from shortcrust, cut pastry about 1 in. wider than pie plate, then fold it back over rim and notch with fingers to give it a firm high edge. Prick the base well with a fork. Mix the eggs with the salt and spice. Gradually stir in the milk and then the pumpkin. Turn all this into the prepared case. Bake in a hot oven, say 450°F, for ten minutes, then lower to moderate, 350°F, and bake for twenty-five minutes, until firm when tested with a knife. Serve with cream if possible.

Pumpkin and Apple Pie

1 lb. pumpkin	*1 lb. peeled and cored apples*
1 egg	*2 tablespoonsful sugar*
Grated rind of 1 lemon	*3 tablespoonsful of water*
1 tablespoonful currants	*Pinch of salt*
2 tablespoonsful milk	

Put alternate layers of apple and pumpkin in a pie dish, sprinkle from time to time with sugar and with currants. Add the water, etc., cover with pastry, and bake in a moderate oven for fifty minutes. (The egg should be beaten in the milk.) Sufficient for three or four people.

Pumpkin Fritters

1 pint mashed pumpkin	*¼ pint milk*
4 tablespoonsful sugar	*1 teaspoonful essence of lemon*
2 tablespoonsful flour	*1 egg*

Mix the pumpkin with the milk, lemon and sugar, adding the flour gradually. Beat together and then add the egg. Beat again for five minutes. Make up into suitable-sized fritters and fry in boiling fat until golden brown. Serve sprinkled with sugar and with sliced lemon. Sufficient for three or four people.

KOHL RABI

The Kohl Rabi looks like a kind of turnip, and has a lovely nutty flavour. It must be quickly grown to be tender, for slowly grown specimens are tough.

Boiled or Steamed Kohl Rabi

Cut off the leaves from the top of the bulb. Cook without peeling, as advised for turnips (see p. 74). Boil or steam until tender and remove the outside skin before serving. Serve with a thick white sauce.

Stewed Kohl Rabi

Peel the roots, quarter them, and place into a saucepan of boiling salted water. Boil until tender. Heat 1 oz. of butter or margarine and stir in gradually ¼ oz. of flour. Add ½ pint of milk and stir until boiling. Sprinkle on a little ground nutmeg and season with pepper and salt. Place in the saucepan the cut-up portions of the root and allow to remain until hot. Serve garnished with parsley or with the tender leaves of the Kohl Rabi itself.

SUGAR PEA

This is the pea the pods of which are also eaten. It is important to pick it just before it is wanted for cooking. If left for about an hour, the skin toughens. Always pick the pods young.

Before boiling, top and tail, like gooseberries.

SALSIFY

A root crop which is called by some the 'vegetable oyster'. It has a delicious 'nutty' flavour and is very easy to grow.

Boiled or Steamed Salsify

Wash the roots and scrape them thoroughly. Drop into water containing lemon juice, to keep the roots white. Cut into lengths 3 in. long and boil or steam until tender. This usually takes about an hour. Drain and serve with a thick white sauce.

Another Method

Wash the salsify in cold water. Place the roots in a saucepan of boiling water, adding a teaspoonful of salt and a teaspoonful of vinegar. Boil for half an hour. Strain, remove the roots, and rub them with a coarse cloth. This removes the skin easily. Cut into portions, return to saucepan, adding a teaspoonful of butter or margarine. Shake over heat until they once more become hot, and serve in a warmed vegetable dish covered with butter sauce or thick white sauce.

Fried Salsify

After cooking and rubbing with a coarse cloth, the cut-up portions of this root may be covered with egg and bread-crumbs or be dipped in batter before being fried.

Salsify Mayonnaise

After cooking and removing the outside skins, allow to get cold, and serve in a salad bowl after cutting up into small portions, and cover with a mayonnaise sauce.

Savoury Salsify

Cook the salsify as already advised and, when tender, place in a pie dish, covering with a thick white sauce. Grate some cheese over the top, add a few breadcrumbs and a pat or two of butter or margarine, and place in a hot oven until the top is beautifully brown.

SCORZONERA

Scorzonera is strangely neglected. De la Quintinye, head of the Royal Gardens in the reign of Louis XIV, described them as one of the most important root vegetables. The roots should never be lifted until just before required. Cook them in their skins, for if peeled first the flavour is poor. The skins can be rubbed off quite easily afterwards. Scorzonera has such a delicate flavour that it should be served merely with melted butter and not a sauce. Freshly lifted roots take under half an hour to cook.

CHAPTER EIGHTEEN

Chutneys—Pickles— Sauces

The making of chutneys, pickles and sauces is very often a grand way of using up fruits and vegetables that might not be quite so suitable for bottling or drying. On the whole, we are a sauce and pickle eating country, and such flavourings do make all the difference to a meal. Chutneys can even be used in sandwiches, being delicious with eggs, for instance. They can also be used for flavouring soups and stews and other cooked dishes, or for eating with fried fish, chops, etc. Many people would not dream of eating curry without chutney.

CHUTNEYS

Tomato and Apple Chutney

3 cooking apples
3 large tomatoes
1 pint vinegar
1½ cups brown sugar
1 teaspoonful mixed peppercorns

2 onions
½ cup stoned raisins
Allspice berries and cloves
1 teaspoonful salt

Peel the apples and chop them finely. Skin the tomatoes, and chop them. Chop the raisins and put all together in a saucepan. Tie the spices in a piece of muslin and add them to the other ingredients. Put the whole mixture over a low heat and simmer gently for 1½ hours. Take out the spice-bag and pack the chutney into jars. Seal and tie down.

Green Tomato Chutney

2 lb. green tomatoes	½ lb. sugar
½ lb. shallots	1½ pints vinegar
1 lemon	1½ lb. apples
½ lb. marrow	½ lb. sultanas
Small piece bruised ginger	1½ oz. salt
¼ oz. chillies	6 peppercorns

Put the sugar into a pan with the vinegar, peppercorns and chillies (tied in muslin), and boil for three-quarters of an hour. Cut all the vegetables into small pieces and add them, and the juice of a lemon, to the vinegar. Simmer gently for three hours, stirring occasionally.

Apple and Onion Chutney

2 lb. apples	2 lb. tomatoes
2 lb. onions	6 oz. sugar
¼ oz. mustard	1 quart vinegar
1 oz. ground ginger	1 oz. salt
1½ lb. sultanas	¼ oz. cayenne pepper

Peel the apples and cut into small pieces. Skin the tomatoes and cut up finely. Peel the onions and chop them. Mix all the ingredients together, put into a pan and simmer over a low heat for 2½ to 3 hours, stirring frequently.

Beetroot Chutney

2 lb. beetroot	1 lb. apples
2 medium-sized onions	1 tablespoonful lemon juice
¼ teaspoonful ginger	1 pint vinegar
½ lb. sugar	½ teaspoonful salt

Boil the beetroot until tender and peel when cold. Cut into small cubes. Peel the onions and apples and cut them up finely. Put them into a pan with the sugar, vinegar, and boil for half an hour. Then add the beetroot and simmer for a further fifteen minutes. Bottle when cold.

Marrow Chutney

2 lb. apples	1½ lb. onions
1 lb. raisins	3 chillies
1 lb. sugar	Cloves
½ oz. ground ginger	Pinch of cayenne
2 lb. marrow	6 peppercorns
½ lb. tomatoes	Salt

Peel the apples, tomatoes, onions and marrow, and cut all into small pieces. Add to the rest of the ingredients and simmer all together for 1½ hours. This chutney should be bottled when quite cold, and will keep for a considerable time.

Turnip Chutney

1 lb. turnips	½ lb. apples
½ lb. onions	6 oz. sugar
¼ lb. sultanas	1 quart vinegar
¼ oz. turmeric powder	Pinch of cayenne
1 teaspoonful mustard	1 oz. salt

Peel the turnips, cut into small pieces, and boil until tender. Peel the onions and chop them finely. Mix the turmeric powder and the mustard to a paste with the vinegar. Mash the turnips and put all the ingredients in a saucepan, simmering over a low heat for one hour, stirring frequently. Do not bottle until cold.

Sweet-Tooth Chutney

2½ lb. tomatoes	2½ lb. sweet apples
2 lb. sugar	2½ pints vinegar
2 onions	2 oz. pickling spice
1 lb. sultanas	1 oz. salt

Peel and finely chop the onions, tomatoes and apples. Tie the pickling spice in a piece of muslin. Mix all the ingredients together and put into a saucepan. Simmer gently for $2\frac{1}{2}$ hours, stirring frequently.

PICKLES

To obtain the greatest success with pickles, the fruits and vegetables should be perfectly dry, fresh and just ripe, but not over-ripe. It is always advisable, when vinegar has to be boiled, to do it in an enamelled pan or, if this is impossible, in a double saucepan. Remember that vinegar is acid and will act on metal vessels. No copper preserving pan should ever be used for the making of pickles, for it is most dangerous.

Pickles have a considerable value dietetically. They are good food and can be used liberally in houses where it is difficult to get fresh fruit or vegetables all the year round.

Beetroot Pickle

4 beetroots	2 onions
10 peppercorns	10 allspice
Sufficient vinegar to cover	Salt

Cook the beetroot and slice thinly. Peel the onions, and cut into rings. Place the beetroot and onion in jars in alternate layers, sprinkling with salt and adding peppercorns and allspice proportionately. Pour the vinegar over the full jars and tie down.

Green Tomato Pickle

2 lb. green tomatoes	4 oz. sugar
1 dessertspoonful mustard	$1\frac{1}{2}$ pints vinegar
$\frac{1}{2}$ oz. mixed spice	Pinch of cayenne
1 teaspoonful curry powder	Salt
2 onions	

Cut the tomatoes into thin slices and sprinkle them lightly with salt. Leave for about 24 hours. Put all ingredients except the tomatoes into a pan and bring to the boil. Add the tomatoes and boil quickly for ten minutes, stirring continually. Bottle when cold.

Apple and Cabbage Pickle

1 lb. firm white cabbage	½ oz. whole pickling spice, tied
1 lb. sour apples	loosely but securely in muslin
½ lb. onions	1 pint vinegar
2 oz. sugar	1 rounded teaspoonful salt

Wash the cabbage and shred; then peel, core and slice the apples and also peel and slice the onions. Put all the ingredients into a pan, cover and simmer for half an hour, stirring occasionally. Take out the spice, but squeeze all the juice from the muslin bag first. Bottle the pickle in the usual way.

Pickled Cucumbers

6 small cucumbers	24 peppercorns
2 quarts of vinegar	2 bay leaves
2 blades of mace	2 oz. salt

Use young, small cucumbers whole. If you only have large ones, cut them into pieces 2 in. long. Put them into an earthenware pan. Sprinkle with salt and let them stand for 24 hours, then pour off the liquid. Wipe the pieces with a cloth. Return them to the dried pan. Boil the vinegar, allowing per quart, 12 peppercorns, one blade of mace, a bay leaf and 1 oz. of salt.

Pour the hot vinegar over the cucumbers and leave for 24 hours. Pour off and boil again. Repeat the process three times. When cold, at the end of the third time, place in a large storage jar. Place over a layer of chopped dill and fennel—then put in another layer of cucumbers. Cover these with another layer of dill and fennel, and so on until the jar is full. Next pour on the vinegar and seal the jar tightly.

Piccalilli

Piccalilli should be made with mixed vegetables—e.g. cauliflower, beans, onions, carrots, gherkins, etc. The vegetables should be prepared, cut into suitably sized pieces, and soaked in a brine (made from 1 lb. salt to ½ gallon of water) for 24 hours. At the end of this time bring the mixture to the boil and cook in the brine until tender. In another pan boil together 2 lb. of brown sugar and 2½ quarts of water. Take a little cold vinegar and thoroughly mix into it half a cupful of flour, ½ oz. mustard and ½ oz. turmeric powder. Add this to the boiling syrup and stir well for five minutes. Then pour it over the vegetables and bottle when quite cold.

Pickled Onions

Peel the onions and pack in a large jar. Pour over them a boiling brine made of 1 lb. salt to ½ gallon of water and leave until cold. Pour off the liquid and bring it to the boil. Pour over again, and again leave until cold.

Pour off and cover the onions with cold vinegar to which has been added a pinch of cayenne, a few peppercorns, a blade of mace, and a bay leaf or a little crushed root ginger.

Pickled Red Cabbage

Trim the cabbage and quarter it. Cut out the stem and slice it very thinly—cross-ways. Place the cabbage thinly on a large dish and sprinkle with salt. Leave for 24 hours. Then drain off as much liquid as possible. Have ready sufficient vinegar to cover the cabbage. Put into a pan, with ½ oz. crushed root ginger and ½ oz. allspice to each quart, and boil up. Pack the sliced cabbage into bottles and pour the vinegar over whilst still very hot. Do not seal until quite cold.

SAUCES

Tomato Sauce

2 onions	1 oz. pickling spice
4 oz. sugar	1 lb. tomatoes
½ pint vinegar	2 cooking apples
½ teaspoonful cayenne	1 teaspoonful salt

Skin the tomatoes and cut into small pieces. Peel and chop the onions and apples. Tie the spices in a piece of muslin and place in a saucepan with the apples, tomatoes and onions. Simmer gently for three-quarters of an hour. Put through a sieve and return to saucepan. Add the vinegar and sugar and boil quickly for about 40 minutes, stirring frequently. Bottle when cold.

Plum Sauce

1½ pints plums
1 lb. sugar
4 oz. currants
¼ oz. chillies
½ teaspoonful grated nutmeg
4 onions

1½ pints vinegar
1 oz. mustard
½ teaspoonful ground ginger
½ oz. allspice
2 oz. salt

To one pint of the vinegar, add the plums, onions and currants. Boil for thirty minutes. Strain and place the liquid in a pan with the rest of the ingredients. Simmer over a gentle heat for about an hour. Bottle when cold.

Nasturtium Sauce

Enough nasturtium flowers to
fill a pint measure
when packed
1 oz. allspice
6 small onions

12 cloves
1 pint vinegar
½ teaspoonful salt
Essence of anchovy

Tie the spices in a piece of muslin. Chop the onions. Place the spices, onion and salt in a saucepan. Add the vinegar and boil for three minutes. Add the flowers and boil again for five minutes. Strain off the vinegar and to each pint add 2 oz. of essence of anchovy.

Mint Jelly (i)

6 lb. apples
4 lemons
½ pint white wine vinegar

2½ lb. sugar
1 large bunch fresh Spearmint
½ bunch of Apple mint

Chop up the apples and cook them to a pulp with a little water to make the juice and to prevent them burning. Strain this juice through a hair sieve. Then boil the liquid for fifteen minutes more before adding the sugar, the juice of four lemons and the white wine vinegar. Stir until the sugar is dissolved. Add the large bunch of fresh mint and the half bunch of Apple mint. Boil until the mint flavour is imparted. Remove the mints and turn the liquid green by using a good vegetable dye. When the jelly sets (test it on a cold saucer) pot it in small jars. Seal when cold.

Mint Jelly (ii)

> 3 cups of minced mint leaves   1½ cups of good vinegar
> 1½ cups of castor sugar   1 lemon
> 1½ oz. powdered gelatine

Wash the fresh mint thoroughly, strip the leaves from the stalks when dry. Melt the gelatine in 3 cups of water. Add the lemon juice. Stir in the vinegar. Add and stir in the sugar until dissolved. Now add the chopped mint and bring to the boil. Simmer for ten minutes, until it gells. Test first on a cold saucer. When ready, add a few drops of green vegetable colouring. Pot in small jars.

APPENDIX

THE VEGETABLES AND THEIR VITAMIN CONTENT

It is the synthetic vitamin which is offered to men and women today and thousands of educated people do not know the difference between the true vitamin produced by nature and those produced by the chemist. The farmer, even the chemically indoctrinated type, does not give his animals synthetic sweetness; he gives them the yeast from the brewers, plus, in fact, the germ of the wheat which we ourselves ought to be eating. We human beings are however surrounded by synthetic foods every day. We buy jams that are dyed artificially and we are unfortunately used to synthetic sweetness.

It is true that the word vitamin is generally known, but is the word enzyme understood or ever thought to be important? Yet there is definite liaison between the two. It is the enzymes which need vitamins as tools to work with, together with the proteins and minerals. The vitamin should of course be in the food you eat and definitely not in a pill. To be truly healthy, the food you eat should be compost grown. Much depends also on how the food is cooked, for to ensure the greatest value from vegetables and salads they should be eaten raw. Grated carrots, grated heart of cabbage, lettuces, radishes, tomatoes, spring onions, parsley, cucumbers, endive and the like are delicious and full of vitamins. It is the over-boiling of the cabbage, swedes, parsnips and other vegetables which does neither them nor you any good.

What are the vitamins that are so important and what do they do?

VITAMIN A

Vitamin A can easily be lost, for instance, by those who use liquid paraffin as a laxative; using fats for frying again and again can cause factor damaging to vitamin A as well. Even the over-use of aspirin can damage the value of the vitamin A intake, I am assured. Please build up the natural vitamin A in your body by eating watercress, spinach, dried apricots, turnip tops, carrots and fishes roe. There is also a valuable amount in eggs, butter, cheese, cod liver oil and liver.

VITAMIN B

The vitamin B complex is now divided up into a number of sub-sections, as it were. B1 can easily be lost in over-boiling vegetables, especially when the water is thrown away. Even the simple fact of toasting bread robs this food of some B1. B2 is the Riboflavin which is found in compost grown vegetables. Cereals and offal are the chief source of vitamin B.

VITAMIN C

Most people know about vitamin C—the Ascorbic acid vitamin. The vitamin that the Government so often wrote about in the war; the blackcurrant vitamin some people have called it. It was given to young people as a juice. Unfortunately it is a vitamin that is not readily stored in the body, but is quickly dissipated in the urine.

Readers should concentrate on providing fresh compost grown fruits and vegetables rather than tinned, processed and preserved ones. Home-grown bottled fruits are a useful addition to winter meals. Vitamin C is found liberally in watercress, strawberries, blackcurrants, sweet peppers, raw broccoli, parsley and Brussels sprouts. Vitamins can easily be 'destroyed' by re-heating foods, by smoking, by adding sugar liberally to stewing fruit and incidentally by the use of saccharine. It is an important vitamin for those suffering from rheumatism or those with low blood pressure.

VITAMIN D

Vitamin D is important as it helps with bone and tooth formation and particularly so for the children. It does help also with fractures in grown ups. Sunlight on the skin helps to produce this vitamin as does the mushroom grown out of doors in the sunshine. The chief sources of vitamin D are cod liver oil, fatty fish, liver, egg yolk and fatty dairy foods. It is a vitamin which is dissipated by liquid paraffin like vitamin A.

VITAMIN E

Vitamin E is an important vitamin. It is not toxic in any way and can hardly be overdone it seems, when naturally occurring. It is of course the fertility vitamin. It can be supplied by the germ of wheat, good 100 per cent whole wheat bread and the compost growth leafy vegetables. Liquid paraffin is a robber of these vitamins, as of course is white flour and high-temperature cookery. It is a particularly important vitamin for those afflicted with arthritis.

VITAMIN K

Vitamin K is necessary for our blood and influences coagulation. It can be found in green vegetables. The intestinal bacteria can play a great part in producing this vitamin but not if chemically produced antibiotics have been taken as medicine. It is an important factor in cases of haemorrhage—because this is the vitamin that assists in the clotting.

It is therefore extremely important in the case of wounds,

low blood pressure, diabetes and excessive menstrual flow. You can receive vitamin K by eating kale and spinach. It is also contained in tomatoes; it is robbed from human beings by liquid paraffin used as a laxative and by synthetic antibiotics.

INDEX

BILL SWAIN

THE COMMONSENSE OF GARDENING

'Answers 574 diverse questions fully and well in a robustly practical way' – *Sunday Telegraph*

YOUR GARDENING PROBLEMS SOLVED!

In this fascinating and informative book, horticultural expert Bill Swain has gathered together 574 of the most vital and frequently posed questions asked by amateur gardeners. From fruit and vegetable growing, soil balance and plant feeding to the propagation of rare shrubs and trees, he gives clear, detailed answers to each individual question, and the result is a thoroughly comprehensive and practical guide to all aspects of gardening. With its wealth of down-to-earth information and a handy, quick-reference index, *The Commonsense of Gardening* is the answer to every gardener's prayer!

'There has never been a book quite like this one, concentrating on the cause of garden problems and their eventual solution . . . a copy should be available to every garden club' – *The Times*

'A wealth of information . . . this will make an ideal guide or present' – *The Observer*

0 7221 8298 8   GARDENING

HYDROPONICS

The latest thing in growing plants – have tomorrow's garden today!

DUDLEY HARRIS

HYDROPONICS – PLANTS WITHOUT SOIL

* Labour-saving
* Virtually weed-free
* Gives bigger and better results

Hydroponics – growing plants without soil in mixtures of essential plant nutrients dissolved in water – is fast becoming popular with flower and vegetable growers everywhere. It is an easy and fascinating method from which flat-dwellers and householders with little or no soil as well as farmers and commercial growers can benefit. In this practical and lucid handbook Dudley Harris explains the principles of hydroponics and describes the equipment necessary for its practice – from an ordinary window box to a concrete tank for the more ambitious grower. Raising seedlings, overcoming pests and diseases, climatic control, irrigation and light requirements are all fully covered. For beginners and more experienced gardeners alike, *Hydroponics* is an invaluable guide to a fascinating new dimension in gardening and agriculture.

0 7221 4340 0   GARDENING & AGRICULTURE

ARABELLA BOXER'S GARDEN COOKBOOK
VEGETABLES FOR VALUE AND VARIETY

With the ever-rising cost of meat and fish, the time has come
to replan our menus and to look again at the wide range of
possibilities in vegetable cookery. For too long the vegetable
has been underrated, a mere accessory to the meat course,
treated with little imagination.

Arabella Boxer's Garden Cookbook elevates the vegetable
to the place it deserves. The aim is to enable the cook not
only to recognise the nutritional value of vegetables, but also
to enjoy their infinite variety. Vegetable flavours change
continually, depending on the season; many can be eaten
raw as well as cooked, and they can be prepared as juices,
salads, soups, casseroles, soufflés, mousses and flans.

In this imaginative yet remarkably practical book,
Arabella Boxer presents over three hundred recipes
ranging from the exotic right down to unusual ways to
prepare the simple potato. In addition, the *Garden
Cookbook* is a comprehensive reference book which
includes virtually every vegetable and herb available from
agar-agar and Brussels sprouts to zucchini.

0 7221 1798 1   COOKING & DINING

All Sphere Books are available at your bookshop or newsagent, or can be ordered from the following address: Sphere Books, Cash Sales Department, P.O. Box 11, Falmouth, Cornwall.

Please send cheque or postal order (no currency), and allow 19p for postage and packing for the first book plus 9p per copy for each additional book ordered up to a maximum charge of 73p in U.K.

Customers in Eire and B.F.P.O. please allow 19p for postage and packing for the first book plus 9p per copy for the next six books, thereafter 3p per book.

Overseas customers please allow 20p for postage and packing for the first book and 10p per copy for each additional book.